Praise For

Braided

"'I knead for my needs,' the author insists—and readers are likely to join her." —*Kirkus Reviews*

"A women's wellness doctor who prescribes the practice of baking bread? I feel like this is exactly the kind of out-of-the-box thinking that is going to save the world right now."
—Jennie Nash, author of *The Victoria's Secret Catalog Never Stops Coming and Other Lessons I Learned From Breast Cancer* and founder of AuthorAccelerator.com

"Beth Ricanati's book is like having coffee with a girlfriend: honest, interesting, and thoughtful. Part memoir, part cookbook, part health guide—but more than all of these, *Braided* is a book that will inspire you to dig deep, think about life, and make challah, maybe even at the same time."
—Ruchi Koval, director of Jewish Family Experience and author of *Conversations with God*

"Some of my favorite moments in teaching American Jewish women's history surround the home and the politics of gender and domesticity—a contemporary space that Beth Ricanati has reclaimed for herself and for all of us through the simple ritual of weekly challah baking. In class, my students discover that contemporary Jewish women can now choose and participate in ancient traditions and rituals in ways that empower them rather than control them. Ricanati's beautifully written story of challah, the joy of creating real food for those we love, and the healing power of being in the moment enlivens this precious inheritance, never more needed than now."
—Marcie Cohen Ferris, professor, American Studies Department, University of North Carolina at Chapel Hill

Braided

Braided

A Journey
of a
Thousand Challahs

Beth Ricanati, MD

SHE WRITES PRESS

Published 2018
Printed in the United States of America
ISBN: 978-1-63152-441-7 pbk
ISBN: 978-1-63152-442-4 ebk
Library of Congress Control Number: 2018937854

For information, address:
She Writes Press
1563 Solano Ave #546
Berkeley, CA 94707

She Writes Press is a division of SparkPoint Studio, LLC.

Book Design by Stacey Aaronson

For David.

And for our children.

TABLE OF CONTENTS

THE RECIPE / 1

INTRODUCTION / 5

DOCTOR'S NOTE: Saved by the Challah / 7

A BRIEF HISTORY OF CHALLAH / 37

MAKING THE CHALLAH: The Journey / 45

IN PREPARATION

⟋ Finding Time *on* Fridays / 47

⟋ Gathering Your Ingredients / 55

⟋ Proofing *the* Yeast / 89

BAKING

⟋ The First Big Mix / 97

⟋ The First Blessing / 101

⟋ Fertilization / 107

⟋ The Second Big Mix / 111

⟋ Kneading *the* Dough / 119

⟋ Rising Up / 123

⟋ The Prayers / 129

⟋ Shaping *the* Dough / 137

⟋ Painting *the* Dough / 145

⟋ Baking *the* Challah / 149

⟋ Rituals Around Eating Challah / 153

CONCLUSION / 159

AUTHOR'S NOTE

In writing this book, I relied on my memories and experiences from medical school, my years as a practicing physician, and a decade of being a challah-maker. In addition, when necessary, I consulted with other experts and researched pertinent facts. To preserve the anonymity of patients and friends mentioned throughout the book, I have changed all names.

THE RECIPE

I share this recipe with a nod to the Jewish Community Center (JCC) in Manhattan, New York City. I have adapted and used this recipe of theirs, which a friend shared with me, since that first time I made challah so long ago. Specifically, she said that it was used in a Mommy and Me cooking class for two- to three-year-olds, and I always figured if these little kids could make challah, then so could I!

2¼ teaspoons loose yeast + 1 teaspoon sugar + 1 cup very warm water (almost too warm, but not hot!)

2 eggs

2 teaspoons salt

¼ cup sugar

⅓ cup oil

4⁺ cups flour

1. Mix yeast, sugar, and warm water together in small bowl; let stand approximately ten minutes. This mixture will start to bubble.

2. Meanwhile, in a large mixing bowl, mix together eggs, salt, sugar, oil, and two cups flour. Now would be a great time to say, "I am making this dough in the merit of _____" (name someone . . . maybe a friend who is sick that week, or someone you are happy for, sad for, mad at, etc.)

3. Add yeast mixture (1) to flour mixture (2).

4. Add approximately 1½ cups of flour to the mixture. Dough should start to form a ball, separating from the bowl.

5. Place the dough on a floured surface and knead, lifting up with one hand and then the other. This should take at least five minutes as dough becomes increasingly elastic. If necessary, add a bit more flour to the dough if still sticky. Knead dough into a ball.

6. Place the dough back into oiled bowl, cover and place the covered bowl somewhere warm for 1–1½ hours to rise; it will approximately double in volume.

7. Preheat oven to 375°. Remove the cover from bowl, place dough on floured surface. Take a small piece of dough (roughly the size of an egg), double wrap in plastic wrap and say the prayer over separating the challah (technically, you're only supposed to say the prayer if more than five pounds of flour are used, but more on that later).* Discard this piece of wrapped dough and continue.

8. Punch out dough one more time. Cut the dough into two balls, one for each challah. Then divide each ball into three equal pieces. Roll out each piece, crimp together at the top and braid into a loaf. Place on a greased cookie sheet. Repeat with second ball of dough. You may let the dough rise again at this step.

9. Paint each challah with a mixture of egg yolk plus a little water.

10. Place braided dough on a greased baking sheet and bake approximately 23–30 minutes, or until bread has risen and is golden brown. Remove, let cool.

11. Place challah on platter, cover and wait for Shabbas dinner. Eat and enjoy!

Baruch Ata A-Do-Nay Elo-haynu Melech Ha-Olam Asher Kidishanu B'Mitzvotav V'Tziyvanu L'Hafrish Challah.

(Blessed are You, Lord, our G-d, Ruler of the Universe, Who has sanctified us with Your commandments and commanded us to separate the Challah.)

INTRODUCTION

For more than ten years now, I have made challah almost every Friday. I have made challah in three different cities, while raising three different children, and trying to keep at least three goldfish alive—alas, unsuccessfully, I must add, for those poor goldfish. I have made challah while mourning the loss of my father, while helping a friend through her cancer diagnosis, and while nursing many a child's wounded knee and wounded pride. I have made challah while working as a busy physician at one of the world's top hospitals and while working as a stay-at-home mom who could never get my kids out the door properly dressed for the bitter Midwest cold. I have made challah alone and with other women—some of them my dearest friends and some I had not even met before we started to bake bread.

Why have I persisted each Friday to make challah for hundreds of Fridays and counting? Because countless demands on my time and energy overwhelmed me. Because one night I even convinced myself that running in place in the upstairs bathroom while I sorted the day's mail counted as exercise. Because as a physician I know all too well that stress like this makes us sick—not just theoretically sick, but actually sick. Because I learned I could *change* this pattern. In taking this time each Friday to sink my hands in a bowl of dough, I learned that I could stop for a half-hour and breathe while I cracked eggs and measured flour. I could stop and make something nutritious and delicious with my own hands and, in the process, I could reconnect with myself and with other women. I could find some happiness in this mixed-up, fast-paced world. I could, in other words, be present—and (drumroll) so can you.

I wrote this story as part memoir, part cookbook, and part manifesto. I wrote this for all the women who are carrying a myriad of responsibilities and not taking even a few minutes to stop and smell the rising yeast. It started for me one Friday morning when it was unclear whether I was going to be OK, and now has sustained me for ten full years. This book is my recipe for how to do it—how to make the bread and take the time you need to take to be truly well. I used to just prescribe medications such as calcium-channel blockers and beta-blockers; now, I also prescribe baking challah.

Don't think you have time to stop for a few minutes and bake bread? Maybe you have a mandatory meeting, a work commitment, a child to pick up, an errand to run. I get all that; I have all that on my calendar, too. But I also know that you can figure this out, and that once you do, you will be amazed at what getting your hands in a bowl of dough each week will do for you. It will impact your body, your spirit, your friendships, and your family. It will get you to slow down, to chill out, to tune in. It will change things at the ex-act level I suspect they need to be changed.

So take a breath, open up your cupboard, get out your bowl, grab the six ingredients, and start mixing.

Oh, and take another breath.

DOCTOR'S NOTE

Saved by the Challah

I had bone-weary, drop-dead, gray-hair-inducing fatigue. Debilitating fatigue. The wake-up-at-4-a.m.-every-morning kind of fatigue. The lost-ten-pounds-and-hadn't-altered-my-diet kind of fatigue. I was so tired that I began to think something was seriously wrong with me.

And I knew about wrong.

My job was to deal with wrong. I was a doctor. I saw all kinds of wrong every day. All the while, I gave my patients advice that I was not following myself. I was a hypocritical mess, if I was honest with myself, headed to exactly the same place that all my patients were headed: to a place where I was disconnected with my body and with my spirit. To the place where disease loves to take hold.

In hindsight, one behavior helped me manage through the chaos, to find a moment of peace, and to propel me forward: making a loaf of white bread. A loaf of a bread called challah, one that I made from scratch, alone in my kitchen one Friday, and then on the following Friday, and again and again for ten years. One thousand loaves of challah and counting. This behavior that helped ground me again—taking time to make challah on Friday—has nothing to do with pills or procedures, magical potions or miraculous surgeries, and everything to do with stopping for a moment to be present in my life.

This is my story. This is the story of how making challah—more specifically, how stopping for a moment once a week—helped me to regain a measure of balance.

Desperate to Make a Difference

My path to overnight gray hair just shy of age forty was years in the making—a lifetime in the making, more likely. Perhaps I could have chosen a different path in high school or in college. Instead, I chose medical school because after years working in hospitals on my summer breaks, participating in women's health initiatives on my college campus, and marching in DC on behalf of women's issues, it just felt like the best way I could make a difference to women and their bodies.

And the first body I got to explore was Ethel's.

Ethel was my assigned cadaver. We named her Ethel and we imagined her as a lovely little dowager. Perhaps a *grande dame* that we might have had tea with seventy-five years ago. White gloves, Meissen china. The four of us met her one morning in our first month of medical school. Or rather, we smelled her first, before we were introduced to her in our anatomy lab. Forget Chanel N° 5; her perfume of choice was formaldehyde. Quickly, it was in my nose, on my clothes, permeating my skin. There lay Ethel, the cadaver who would teach us her secrets over the next year.

She slowly revealed herself to us. A leg here, a muscle there. Such long fingers. Did she play piano? Shriveled tissue-paper skin. Tell me, Ethel. Tell me how you got those wrinkles?

Did you have a lover? Did you hide during the War? Did you want to be more than your gender allowed you to be?

We worked on her, with her, throughout that first year of medical school. Inside, she looked just like the textbooks said she would. That simple fact surprised me each time we pulled back the plastic wrap to begin another anatomy lab. Here's a drawing of a heart on page 85 (Moore's *Clinically Oriented Anatomy*, 1992). Drawn to perfection. Look, study; memorize the four chambers, the left anterior descending artery. *Oh look*, Ethel's got the same one, too! We easily sought out her four heart chambers, her left anterior descending artery.

She was so little, her bones fragile as egg shells. And so thin—it was easy for the four of us to work together around her, passing instruments as we needed them back and forth across her to each other. Our group of four peered into her abdominal cavity. Four modern women. Four women *medical students*. Were we better than Ethel? Had she fought the good fight for us gals?

And there it was. Such a tiny thing, really; maybe the size of a pear. Bosc or Anjou, you decide. Wars fought over this little thing, really? The body politic. For this tiny thing, really? It was so little. Her uterus. And there it fit, right in the palm of my gloved hand. I think I half-expected it to weigh me down, literally. This small and extremely light-weight organ I gingerly held in my palm was the reason I had gone to medical school in the first place. The reason I had marched three times in Washington, DC, during college. The reason my father had deigned to call me emotional, moody. *Just a girl.*

I don't know, my father has now been gone for a few years, and maybe, just maybe, I will admit sometimes, late at night and alone with my thoughts, that he was right. I guess I can fairly easily imagine the picture he saw, even though I took the requisite classes he, my mother, and my academic advisors had picked out for me in high school—the classes that I hadn't appreciated most of the time. I guess I can imagine it: the outwardly bored, sometimes moody teenager he saw.

I spent too much time then staring out the overly large, single-paned windows at my midwestern boarding school. I spent time sneaking down to the deserted parking lot a few blocks off campus to smoke cigarettes with an older boy. He was smarter than me; I liked his ideas better than my own. Not a great confidence-builder. My best girlfriend didn't even live to see us graduate high school. The same girl who shared tomato soup with me at an off-campus restaurant the day the Space Shuttle Challenger exploded. The silence in the restaurant was deafening, save for the desperate voice on the radio. She had depression before I knew there was such a diagnosis, and her death shocked me; it wasn't fair, I didn't get to laugh with Meredith through those last difficult years of school. No boy talk, no college talk. Why didn't doctors understand girls like her?

It was Meredith who helped me begin to see that I might be more than just a girl.

Our freshman year, she was in the school infirmary during Passover, the Jewish holiday that commemorates the Jews' freedom from slavery in ancient Egypt. I could count the number of Jewish students at my boarding school on my fingers. We started each day with Chapel. The large wooden cross, suspended high above the altar, stared down at me, making me wonder what a Jewish girl was doing there at 8 a.m. every morning. The boys slouched in the hard wooden pews, their blazers haphazardly hanging off their shoulders; the girls trying to be something they weren't quite ready to be.

That year, in that non-Jewish environment, I decided to "observe" Passover. One doesn't so much observe Passover as live Passover, with all its rules and stipulations, but what did I know then? I thought it only meant not to eat bread—specifically any yeast products—for eight days. I've learned since then that there are actually five forbidden grains that can't be eaten that week: wheat, barley, oats, rye, and spelt. In addition, we don't eat *chametz*, foods that have been leavened by yeast or alcohol. The Ashkenazi Jews (the branch that I am from) don't eat rice, legumes, and corn, as well. Now, so many years later, I've taken to claiming my husband's Sephardic heritage, since the Sephardim are allowed rice. Sushi never looked so good.

So Saturday morning of that week, I went to visit my friend tucked away in the infirmary, down a few steps, beneath one of the boys' dormitories. Down the long hall I tiptoed, peeking in the open doorways, looking for her telltale long blond hair. And there she was, in the last room, bent over her breakfast tray. She didn't look up when I said hi. So I picked up a piece of her buttered toast and took a bite. That got her attention, and I broke my Passover observance without even being aware of it.

She was in and out of the infirmary the rest of that year. I didn't really understand why. I knew that she had physical symptoms—pain and difficulty walking. I didn't realize the connection to her emotional health, and no one clued me in. I wonder now if they even knew what was really wrong with her. We know so much more now about mental health. When I miss Meredith now, I like to think that my children and their friends will have it easier, that at least if they need help, it might actually be there for them.

One hot summer night, my mom came slowly down our upstairs hallway with that *look* on her face. You know the one. The one where you wish you could roll the clock back a few minutes, press "reset" and start over. Meredith was dead. Just like that. A fatal complication with her medications, so I was told. I wonder about that diagnosis. I had written to her while she was away at summer camp—a letter about all the usual summer stuff, and to find out how she was feeling; yet it turns out I didn't know how she truly felt. And now I never would.

I couldn't save her. I couldn't even help her.

That's an awful feeling.

I think of her some years at Passover, when I am perhaps on day six of eight and trying to be mindful not to eat yeast. It's hard. And that buttered toast I nabbed off her breakfast tray so long ago tasted so *good*.

The Luck of the Draw

In the spring of my senior year, I got accepted to the University of Pennsylvania. My family, I think, was shocked. My sister and brother are both very bright by all definitions. They had high grades, and were early members of their class's cum laude societies. My sister, who is older than my twin brother and me by two years, was already attending an Ivy League institution by this time. My twin brother, in addition to being one of the top in his class academically, was also an incredible runner. He would go on to run competitively in college for four years and then qualify for the Boston Marathon.

And then there was me.

In the majority of my classes, I was bored. I didn't have any study habits to speak of, having jumped schools every two years prior to high school. And the common refrain, "Beth just doesn't apply herself . . . if she would just apply herself . . ." unfortunately had the unintended consequence of reinforcing my lack of interest in school.

I had spent the summer before my freshman year of high school living in Europe with two different families, an experience that I had arranged myself. I spoke passable French and fancied myself a Parisienne. I wandered aimlessly through the Jeu de Paume museum alone. Impressionist paintings hanging there particularly attracted my interest.

I attended the bar mitzvah of the grandson of a French woman with whom I was staying, an affair so extraordinary I still remember almost every detail. The dress I wore was not flattering—actually, it was a pale, dove-gray and white cotton top with a matching skirt. No one looks good in a full-pleated skirt, but certainly no fourteen-year-old girl in the throes of a changing body. And then there was the synagogue itself. I had never been to a synagogue where the women sat separately from the men. We sat upstairs, and the women around me talked for the entire service, animated and engaged with each other, and occasionally with their prayer books. The altar of the synagogue, La Victoire, faced east toward Jerusalem. Also known as the Great Synagogue of Paris, La Victoire was built in 1874, financed in part by the famed Rothschild family; it was the largest synagogue in France. I loved that the sanctuary faced east, and at that moment, all over the world, Jews faced Jerusalem. I felt connected, a sense of belonging that I hadn't even realized I lacked.

Later that summer, this same bar mitzvah boy, his family, and I went on a driving trip from Paris, up through Bavaria, then east, over to Vienna. We sped through the countryside in their large BMW, the backseat so spacious that the two children and I never touched. Approaching the German border, Monsieur pulled the car over, unscrewed the central piece of the steering wheel and placed a large amount of cash inside the hollow center. "*Et voila,*" he said as he winked at his children and me, "Screw those Germans." And the five of us, four French Jews and one American Jew, easily crossed the border into Germany.

During our entire week in Bavaria, I couldn't bring myself to get near a shower. Years earlier, when I was ten, I had been obsessed with Anne Frank and stories of children in World War Two. I realized that even though it was forty years later, and that it is not fair to hold this generation culpable for the past generation's atrocities, even looking at a shower made me ill.

I took a lot of baths that week.

Monsieur called my father, had a short conversation, and quickly passed the phone to me. A transatlantic call in 1984 was a big deal. I spoke to my parents less than a handful of times that summer. The purpose of that particular call: to inquire if my dad would be okay if we visited Dachau. With a simple yes from my dad, who had probably never visited Dachau, or Auschwitz, or Buchenwald, I found myself in the parking lot of a concentration camp. I was just shy of fifteen; Anne Frank had been fifteen when she died at Bergen-Belsen concentration camp, also in Germany. I did not mind watching the younger children outside the camp gates while the adults went inside. Why was it sunny that day? Why was I free to play outside the walls, with no Jewish star affixed to my red and white striped t-shirt? How did I get to be so lucky?

Luck may be the intersection of chance and preparedness, but on that day, I just felt plain, good old-fashioned, random luckiness for being born in a different time, a different country.

Doing Well and Doing Good

Later that summer, I flew back home to Ohio, turned fifteen, and showed up with all the wrong clothes at my new boarding school in a small town. I didn't have the proper currency to handle boarding school easily: I didn't play field hockey well; I placed into French 3 with the upperclassmen instead of lowly French 1 with my classmates; and my father was a member of the board of trustees, so there was the lingering question of whether I had even gotten in on my own merit in the first place.

That's when I wrote my first book, a cookbook.

I wish that I could say my reasons for writing it were purely altruistic—but it wasn't. I wish I could say that writing a cookbook had always been my destiny—but it hadn't. I wish that I could say any number of flattering things—but I can't. The cookbook was just one example of one of my favorite truisms in life: you can do well, and you can do good, and you can do them *at the same time.*

I needed to go to college. Preferably a good one. That was a given in my family, like making your bed and emptying your trashcan and putting down the toilet seat each and every morning. And I wanted to go to an Ivy League school. I was, in fact, obsessed with it. Why? Because it looked good. I noticed the way that people nodded their heads a certain way at my sister—perhaps with a bit more respect, perhaps with a knowing glint. It's crass; it's judgmental; it's egotistical. And I wanted it. But first I had to get in.

Many years earlier, in second grade, I became fascinated with blind people when we learned about Helen Keller. I insisted on learning Braille. In high school, I had the thought to do something for the visually impaired and blind. I approached Stouffer's, headquartered just outside of Cleveland, and the Cleveland Society for the Blind during my freshman year of high school with the idea of modifying some of Stouffer's frozen food recipes. Developing the cookbook allowed me to do something nonacademic, to create something. Working on this allowed me permission to leave campus, to attend meetings at the Stouffer's headquarters just a short drive from school. The process took several years, and I was involved from start to finish. This cookbook let me succeed at something that was my own—and very different from what my siblings were doing. At the start of college, when the provost of the university recognized eight students at our opening convocation, including the "girl in the incoming class of 1992 who spent years creating a cookbook for the blind," I knew why I was there.

College began well enough, until the family's enthusiasm

began to dim when I announced on a visit home that I wanted to study art. I am not a spreadsheet kind of gal. I just know inside when something strikes me, and art did. I did try to assuage the impulse with courses in history (excellent for law school, the direction my older sister was headed), English (maybe junior editor at *Vanity Fair*? Or at least a reason to get to New York—the city that I had wanted to move to since I began subscribing to *Architectural Digest* at age ten), but I always came back to art. I couldn't resist sitting in a darkened lecture hall, lost in a modern architecture survey course, or in a small seminar studying Cézanne. I chose art for myself and, years later in anatomy class in my first year of medical school, I realized how fortuitous that decision had been: studying art taught me to *see* things nobody else saw, and it helped me save women's lives.

Sitting in a darkened lecture hall is good for many things, including nursing hangovers and checking out the cute curly-haired guy, a junior, with the leather jacket and day-old scruff, sitting two rows up, three seats to the left. And just as important—maybe more so, depending on how intellectual I felt like being at the moment—sitting in a darkened lecture hall looking at art better prepared me for medical school and my career as a clinician than any premed class. Why? It's simple. The assignment was always a variation on a theme: write something about what you see up on the screen. Maybe it works once to be literal. Maybe you can describe the Renaissance painting by Agnolo Bronzino, *An Allegory with Venus and Cupid*, as a beautiful painting and leave it at that; or, as several scholars have noted, you can say that the painting instead contains a veiled reference to King Francis I of France and his losing battle with syphilis. Cosimo I de Medici, Duke of Florence and later Grand Duke of Tuscany, presented the painting to the king several years before the king's death. This clever Italian ruler likely knew exactly what Bronzino had painted: images of syphilis pop up throughout the painting, including the telltale physical symptoms of hair loss, poor dentition, lack of fingernails and gnarled fingers. None of this is readily apparent, and had someone not pointed it out to me, I probably wouldn't have looked for it either. You have to start to look, really look. And that requires learning *how* to look. I spent hours looking at works of art up on the screen, describing them literally and figuratively.

Later on, these lessons that I learned in darkened lecture halls were precisely what I needed to draw upon when taking care of patients. I had to see beyond the Arab woman as she sat adjacent to me and whispered of her husband's demands. I had to *see* her life to help her—a culture far different from my own. She sat there, wholly covered from head to toe. Did she know I was Jewish? I loved getting to ask her all those juicy personal questions, both as a woman and as a Jew. It almost felt subversive. We got through the preliminary Review of Systems quickly and efficiently: no cardiac, pulmonary, GI (gastrointestinal), or musculoskeletal symptoms. No visual, hearing, or other neurological symptoms. Then I hit paydirt. I routinely asked the following questions of all my patients, and I strategically asked them last. I wanted to normalize these sensitive topics, make them no more or no less important than asking about her heart or her lungs or her vision. I asked about seatbelts and guns. You'd be surprised how many people—with kids—live with guns and don't lock the bullets up separately. And then I asked her about disordered eating, careful not to use any labels such as anorexia or bulimia, and I asked her about living in an unsafe environment, again careful with my word choice. I inquired about her sexual health. The translator just looked at me. She had already been looking askance at me throughout the interview, clearly indicating that some of my questions were not of the usual variety. But since I believe our health is dependent upon both our physical and mental well-being, I asked the translator to pose these questions, too.

Finally the Arab woman spoke. She spoke of sleepless nights and depressed moods. She spoke of perimenopausal symptoms and tension with her husband. And we got to the heart of the matter, to what was really bothering her emotionally as well as physically. The official reason listed on the chart for her visit had read: *CheckUp.* Just a routine checkup as long as her husband was in town for treatments.

A routine checkup—that couldn't have been further from reality. There was nothing routine about her visit, except that she was like so many of my other perimenopausal and menopausal patients—dealing with hot flashes, night sweats, poor sleep, memory loss, and changes in libido. But she was dealing with so much more; she was dealing with a husband and his illness. She was dealing with her changing relationship with not only herself at this stage in her life, but also with a changing relationship with her husband—perhaps as a result of her own perimenopause or perhaps a result of his illness, or more likely a result of both of them. And she was dealing with this in a country that had very strict mores for women. Clearly a difficult time for her.

Ultimately, she let me examine her, and go on to treat her.

Little did I know then that those years spent studying art would be so valuable. Little did I know that really learning to look, in this case past my patient's full-body coverup, would yield so much more to her story. Fortunately, she was willing to try some of the lifestyle modifications we discussed that day, as well as a low-dose medication for her symptoms; and when her husband needed to come back for treatments, she flew in to see me, this time with a smile on her face, and a lightness to her gait.

A Profession for the Hyperorganized

Back on my college campus, everything changed one day on a dare. My history genius friend told me, late one night, that she was contemplating medical school. *Medical school*, my mind shouted at itself! *What a great idea! Why hadn't I thought of that, too?* At the same time I was studying art history, I had also been spending my summers working in hospitals with a variety of clinical researchers. I don't know why it clicked that night, but my friend's random, offhand comment inspired me and soon I found myself constructing models of chemical molecules in the killer of all premedical school classes: organic chemistry.

It's not right and it's certainly not fair—in fact, it smacked of misogyny—but when I announced I was going to medical school, everybody treated me differently. All of a sudden, the combination of art history and organic chemistry sounded brilliant. Those molecular models really are beautiful, and if you look carefully, the logic of their construction can become so clear. This all with no AP science in high school, and not a single science class until the tail end of my college life.

I finished my premedical requisite classes, took the MCAT examination, and applied to medical school. I attended a good school and trained at wonderful hospitals, both in Cleveland and New York City. The medical life is one that demands precision and order, everything laid out step-by-step in front of you. The classes I took followed the core systems of the body, and the training had a wonderfully disciplined rhythm and symmetry to it. In particular, I was always a member of a team, and my role was clear and defined down to the length of my white coat.

My plan early on in medical school centered on becoming a breast surgeon. After all, I had gone to medical school with the express purpose of helping women, and as a breast surgeon, I could have a direct impact on women's health, both in the general sense and individually. Breast cancer runs on both sides of my family; nationally, one in eight women will be diagnosed with breast cancer in her lifetime. (Many women I know already have been diagnosed with this disease.) I longed to help, and becoming a breast surgeon held great appeal. Besides, I discovered that I really liked this particular surgery. It is short and sweet, often just using local anesthesia, and with minimal blood loss.

As a third-year medical student, I got to practice my suturing skills. And practice and practice and practice. First, I could be found walking around the hospital with a string of suturing material always stuck in one of my pockets, practicing my knots wherever and whenever. I attached the string to the top of the stack of papers that I perpetually carried in one pocket or another. Like my mother before me, who always brought her knitting to meetings, I found myself bemused as I practiced my suturing knots while sitting in rounds. And while sitting in conferences. And while walking up and down the hospital corridors. I became really good that year, first at tying knots and then at sewing a neat little line of stitches. No ugly scars for my patients. It was really important to me that these women have as tiny a physical scar as possible. Art is beautiful, remember. Their scars should be beautiful, too.

I ended up not becoming a surgeon. After learning that I'd first have to complete a general surgery residency (five long years) and then would still need to complete a breast surgery fellowship (two more years), I thought better of my breast surgery plan. I wanted children, a family. I had read *Ms. Magazine*, I had marched in Washington, and I had believed I could do and be anything. Finally, in the middle of medical school, I realized that I could not do and be anything without a cost. I would have to get at women's health from another approach. I chose internal medicine, a specialty that would allow me the opportunity to learn about the entire body, how every system works. I would learn about their reproductive systems and their hearts and their lungs and their kidneys. I would know how their hormonal systems work and their GI tracts. I would know all of it.

This profession was designed for hyperorganized people —people like me. I liked to play it like a chess match, always looking about four moves ahead. My daughter's soccer coach exhorts his players to "run to where the ball is *going*, not to where it is." I like to think that's what I was doing at that time. In the spring of the second year of my internal medicine residency program, the chief residents distributed the schedule templates for the next year, our third and final year as residents. They instructed us to rank-order our preferences. How would we prefer to complete our third year requirements? Months of working on the various hospital wards, managing the interns and medical students on our team while simultaneously taking care of patients? Working shifts in the ER? Taking care of patients in various outpatient clinics? Some of these rotations were harder than others; some required me to be in the hospital overnight, some perhaps working just nights for several weeks in a row. Some were just downright exhausting. We'd have to do them all, but at least we had somewhat of a choice as to when we did each rotation.

That little voice in my head was loud, insistent. It reminded me to think of others first, not myself. So that's what I did. I purposely rank-ordered the worst schedule first, because it meant that the end of my third year would be easier and I wouldn't be putting any undue burden on my colleagues by having to miss any difficult rotation. I wanted to get pregnant that year; I just didn't want to piss anyone off in the process.

Of course, I got that worst possible schedule. The one I had chosen. I should have been in my element, taking care of others first, either my patients at work or the other residents. Except then I actually got pregnant. I spent the first part of that third year chugging 7 Up, and secretly getting sick in almost every bathroom on every floor of the hospital. All the while, I didn't let it slow me down. I was running around, just hoping to survive the eighty-hour workweek. Yet I almost never appreciated the wonder that was my life. A first pregnancy. The completion of a difficult and rewarding residency-training program. Living in a city that never slept.

I finished my residency and took my internal medicine board examinations. With my four-month-old baby in tow, I flew back to my hometown to take the two-day exam. Handing my baby off to my mother was the only way I could figure out how to get appropriate around-the-clock childcare so I could complete the examination. Others showed up to the large sterile conference room to take the test with textbooks in hand, ostensibly to cram a few more arcane facts in during the break. They toted books; I toted a breast pump so I could dash off every few hours and pump breast milk for my first-born. I believed my children should not have infant formula in their first year. Needless to say, from that day on, I became the master of sneaking off to pump breast milk—anywhere, anytime.

I began practicing, first at The Center for Women's Health at Columbia Presbyterian in New York City. When we moved back to Cleveland, I joined the Women's Health Center at the Cleveland Clinic. It was an innovative multidisciplinary center where women obtained comprehensive health care all in one facility. I could palpate a breast lump in one of my patients and then moments later walk her just a few doors down the hallway, still in her hospital gown, and arrange for a mammogram that day—and, if needed, to see a member of the breast cancer team. I could see something abnormal on a pelvic exam and have a gynecologist step into the exam room right then and there for a consultation. I loved how thorough it all was, and how efficient. Who has time to keep coming back to the doctor, with children to pick up from school and meetings to attend to and a garden to water?

And it was prestigious—the external validation mattered to me. I had always managed to be at the best institutions possible. I had been on a mission—a fast-paced, ambitious mission—for most of my entire life. I may not have always wanted to go to medical school, but I had in fact been choosing to help others from a very early age. What I still hadn't learned yet, even as I began to build my medical practice, was that it didn't have to be so black or white. I still hadn't learned that I could help others and help myself, too.

Moms Who Eat Bread

My practice in women's health care at the Cleveland Clinic was divided roughly into three disparate areas: younger women patients, in their twenties to early forties, who came to see me for "benign gyn" issues; postmenopausal women; and women with eating disorders such as anorexia, bulimia, binge eating—the whole spectrum of disordered eating. In the standard-of-care three-way approach to managing eating disorders, I was the medical doctor that complemented the nutritional and psychological support that these women required. After all, despite what most people believe—what I believed until I knew better, and even these women with disordered eating themselves believed—eating disorders aren't just measured by how much a patient weighs, by a number on a scale. They're measured in a patient's erratic heart rate, which may be too slow or irregular. They're measured in missed or irregular periods. They're measured in depressed and anxious moods. They're measured by changes to *every* system in a patient's body.

Eating disorders have fascinated me since adolescence. This aberrant behavior has alternately intrigued and repulsed me since I hid out in my dormitory room that one semester I went to school in England. I was twelve years old, the oldest girl in the dormitory. The only one who wore a bra. I was the *American*. The one who didn't know any world geography or Latin or French. But I knew where to procure the Cadbury chocolate bars. And I knew when the other five girls who shared my room in the "Cottage" with me would be out.

I gained over ten pounds that spring in England.

Fortunately, my flirtation with disordered eating remained just that, a flirtation. I remember girls in my high school dormitory with florid eating disorders—I couldn't understand them and their behavior then, couldn't grasp that they could restrict themselves to a diet of carrots and hundreds of abdominal crunches, and yet their dedication and focus to their illness held me in awe. I wanted to succeed at something, too.

Weight and body image dominated my life for a long time. I can tell you exactly what I weighed when I started ninth grade, when I graduated high school; I can tell you what I weighed when I fled to a friend's apartment in college to study for finals and subsisted on raw vegetables and Diet Coke for three days. I can tell you what I weighed when I fell in love for the first time. But, fortunately, I can no longer tell you what I weigh now. Having children changed that for me. My body was integral to their creation, and to their subsequent nourishment for the first year of each of their lives—

and overnight I gained a new, different perspective. I became in awe of my body and what it could do. Treating women with disordered eating became an extension of that—to help them, hopefully, also realize the wonder that is *them*, that is *their body*.

One day, one patient with an eating disorder told me a story that I still find myself thinking of at the oddest moments, like when I am packing lunch for my children or debating with myself whether I really want to eat breakfast on a particular morning. Some people's stories resonate more powerfully than others; some have the power to actually change my behavior. Hers is one such story.

This woman always made her children a homemade meal each morning and explained that they must eat breakfast, that it was the most important meal of the day. She told them that breakfast equaled *break*-the-fast—that this meal revved their dormant metabolisms, got them going for the day. When she had been sick, she herself did not eat breakfast, and did not eat any bread products, any "carbs," as she liked to tell me. Except in secret, except when she binged behind closed doors. And thus, her young daughter had assumed, had truly believed, that all mothers did not eat any bread products. One day when she was better, this mother began to eat bread again. Those dreaded carbs, no longer so dreaded. And she ate breakfast again. And one morning at breakfast, her daughter noticed her eating toast.

"Mommy," her daughter asked, "I didn't know that moms could eat bread. Are you okay?"

Are you okay?

The lesson hammered home that day for me? Our children

are watching us. Always watching us, absorbing our actions. Forget what we tell them; it's what we *do* that matters.

The Truth in My Own Behavior

And the truth? What so many of us women do is not really all that healthy all the time. For a long time, as I built my practice, I refused to see this truth in my own behavior. But I saw it in my patients' bodies and I heard it in their words time and time again.

After all, I had looked under my patients' hospital gowns, I had heard their heartbeats, I had listened to their stories. When I had completed her physical examination—regardless of why she had come to see me in the first place, be it for anorexia, cancer, depression, diabetes, or anything else—we would talk about the patient's life: her stress, her eating, her not having enough time for exercise. I saw so many women, so many of them filled with stress and sadness. Their behaviors were so unhealthy. And stress and sadness, coupled with unhealthy behaviors, can kill people. It really can. And it really does.

I saw it with my own two eyes: a middle-aged patient came in late one afternoon. She was so frustrated that before we had even begun to discuss the reason for her visit, she cried. Her "regular" physician didn't get it, she complained. Something was wrong. She knew it. They always know it. They always told me what's wrong with them. And they were always right. So there this woman sat, in a hospital gown that didn't properly cover her, perched on the end of the exam table, where the flower-patterned paper covering the table ripped under her weight. You see, she was obese. So her regular doctor missed that rock-hard blob she and I both felt in the folds of her abdominal girth. That rock-hard blob would be her death knell: she had advanced metastatic ovarian cancer.

She died later that year. I never saw her again, having immediately referred her to a gynecological oncologist (a doctor specializing in cancers such as ovarian and uterine) for treatment. We spoke on the phone once, after she had started a palliative treatment regimen. She sounded resigned, sad, and grateful to be pain-free. I hung up the phone and cried in my windowless office, tucked beneath the stairs of a large, nondescript hospital building. I felt as though I, and the whole medical system, had somehow failed her, though I knew rationally that wasn't the case. I felt as though somehow, if she had been diagnosed sooner, she might have lived. I wanted to be mad at her "regular" doctor for missing the diagnosis, but I really wasn't. Ovarian cancer is horrible. Women present late with symptoms, making successful treatment difficult.

In the face of all this sickness and stress, I kept practicing medicine as I had been trained to do. But listening to the patients' histories, doing the requisite examinations, and prescribing the medications wasn't enough. More and more, I felt inadequate. I felt that I wasn't doing enough. But there was scant time for self-reflection. I had children to raise, a career to master. Like so many women I knew and so many other women I didn't know, I juggled myriad responsibilities. I was a physician, a mother, a daughter, a wife, a friend—always busy. Being busy meant little time to actually be present. I was always over *there* when I should have been over *here*. But busy was good—or so I thought. I had managed to act out a rather successful life, so why stop now?

Occasionally I dropped the ball. Sometimes that was all right, like forgetting to pick up the dry cleaning on my way home from work, like forgetting to sign some form or another at one of my children's schools, like forgetting to water the geraniums that I had just planted that weekend, with pots and pots of white flowers soon to wilt. Sometimes dropping the ball really wasn't all right at all, like the time I was sitting in my child's parent-child Hebrew class, supposedly learning a prayer together but instead reviewing silently in my mind the five o'clock meeting that I had just abruptly left. Itching to surreptitiously glance at my Blackberry, I sometimes did just that, sliding my hand quietly down my side, into my open bag, hoping no one would notice, especially the stern teacher in her stylish pantsuit at the front of the room—the one who knew exactly what I was up to and kept sending scathing glances in my direction as I punched silently on the buttons. I was not exactly the role model I wanted to be for my child at that moment, but I was unable to resist the allure of the tasks that still had to be done back at the office. And here's the price I paid for not resisting: now, a few years later, my child chants the prayer beautifully, and I do not. I do not know it. I missed the opportunity to learn it with my child. I helped somebody else at the expense of helping my child. Actions always speak louder than words: our children absorb and learn by watching us, not necessarily listening to us. And I was not present; I did not learn the prayer. And I can't let that go.

As I continued racing around, what I believed unconsciously was that I didn't need to take care of myself to still be able to take care of others, that I was somehow immune from the diseases and sadness I saw in my patients each day. So I kept moving, dashing between patient visits and school pick-ups and Target runs in our hideous utilitarian minivan that I had vowed never to purchase in the first place, just trying to hold it together, in a constant real-world *Caps for Sale* story. It was controlled chaos. I couldn't stop, and I wasn't sure I even wanted to stop. I liked it, that frenetic pace. By this time, I should've owned stock in Advil. I had bottles stashed in my car, in my top right desk drawer at work, in my purse, and throughout our house. Take two Advil and call me in the morning. At least in this, I followed my own prescription. I had figured out that gel caps reached my headaches faster than tablets and I even went so far as to think that I was clever for making this discovery.

Munching on an apple in the car, driving one-handed on the way into work does not make for a nutritious break-fast—even if the apple is crisp and organic. Cereal and nuts eaten from a Ziploc bag at my desk do not make for a suffi-cient lunch—even if the cereal is plain shredded whole wheat, the nuts cashews. There were occasions during this frenetic time when my three children were all in elementary school and I still tried to meet the American Heart Association (AHA) guidelines for exercise each day—the same recom-mendation that I spent time explaining to my patients daily. Why? A minimum of ten thousand steps a day is a great way to help reduce the risk of heart disease. And what so many women still don't realize is that heart disease is our number-one killer. I wanted to reduce my odds.

And so I strove to walk those ten thousand steps each and every day myself. But by the end of some days during that time, I hadn't met my goal. It's difficult to walk that much sitting at a desk most of the day. It takes effort; it takes forethought. Sometimes the hour grew late, maybe 11 p.m., the children all tucked in bed, the homework all done, and I still hadn't hit that magic ten-thousand-step mark according to my cute little pedometer. I wasn't going to go walk the neighborhood and risk a run-in with a raccoon. Instead, I grabbed the stack of mail, which hadn't been dealt with, and stood there in my bathroom and ran in place while I discarded Sears washing machine ads, scanned bank statements, and made sure that nothing earth-shattering had been delivered to our mailbox that day. In my troubled mind, this counted as something good that I did for myself. And approximately twenty-two minutes later, my pedometer clocked in at ten thousand steps.

All good—or so I thought then.

I couldn't carve out time to get to the gym—never mind that I don't like gyms in the first place. It took too long to drive there, exercise, shower, and get home. I couldn't get up early in the morning to take a walk; there were school lunches to pack and breakfasts to make and children to wake. I couldn't find time after work and before dinner. It was too dark outside or too cold or too wet, and there was homework to help with, dinner to prepare. Instead, for a few years, I convinced myself that running in place for twenty to thirty minutes at night in the bathroom constituted *exercise*. If I felt extra zippy, I might actually run back and forth between the bathroom and the bedroom for a little variety. Every few days I added hand weights to the routine. Childhood memories of my grandmother's physician's description of her brittle bones after her hip shattered continued to haunt me. So I did five different arm exercises, ten repetitions each. I repeated that routine three times. Somehow I thought this might ward off the specter of osteoporosis.

Running in place in my bathroom late at night while sorting the day's mail may constitute physical movement, but this was not a healthy and sustainable method of exercise. And I looked ridiculous. But this running in place enabled me to continue my fast pace, my hyphenate role of doctor-mom-room parent-wife-daughter.

Challah Comes Calling

And then came the call that jolted me out of my stupor.

It was all so innocent, just a phone call to check in with a friend. This friend, Alexa, challenged me to make my own challah that year. She had been my friend and neighbor when we lived in New York City. I was living in the Midwest by then, devoted to my work at the Cleveland Clinic. I'm not even sure how challah came up in that conversation, though I knew that Alexa baked her own. I, however, did not bake. Anything. Except boxed brownies, which had been a specialty of mine since seventh grade advisory class Thursday afternoons. I baked them to impress a boy in my advisory; how clichéd, right, to bake for a guy? But there you have it. I still like to bake for my man; some things never change. As for the brownies, Ghirardelli brownie mix has replaced the classic Betty Crocker mix; otherwise that specialty of mine remains the same.

I certainly didn't bake anything then as complicated as bread, let alone challah. I had a bread machine from Williams-Sonoma in my basement that was gathering dust as Alexa and I spoke that day. My husband and I had put it on our wish list for a wedding gift, thinking, I suppose, of our fantasy life—and most definitely not of our real life.

But it was strange, almost inexplicable, how Alexa's exhortation spoke to me that year. I had to try to make challah. I simply had to. *It was time for me to change.*

Alexa promised that it was simple. Mix six ingredients in a bowl and put it in the oven. Bread just comes together on its own, or so she implied.

But, as with so many things, it turned out that it wasn't so simple. I called my friend quietly from the third aisle in the grocery store, needing help with what kind of yeast to buy. I concealed the phone and whispered, embarrassed that I didn't know. Couldn't there just be *one* brand of yeast, one kind? I realized standing in that aisle just how little I knew.

I called her again at least four times later that afternoon in my kitchen, as I added the ingredients to the bowl. Did the order I added them to the bowl matter? Just how warm should the water be for the yeast? How many bubbles did it need? And how would I know when it was kneaded enough? And how did you knead, again?

"You'll know," my friend said. She was talking about trust, about faith, about patience. She was talking about being present.

It had been a very long time since I had been present. I feared I had lost the ability, and that day in my kitchen, I was trying to get it back. With my hands steeped in the dough, I felt I *could* actually slow down and step off that flying carousel, even if just for a few minutes. Finally, after much hand-holding and telephoning back and forth, I got the lopsided challah braids into the oven.

The aroma that enveloped our house a half-hour later nearly rendered me speechless. My house was suddenly a home. Two golden loaves graced the old warped baking sheet. I let out a breath I didn't realize I had been holding. My shoulders dropped, the tension cradling my head eased up a bit.

That night, we gathered around my new creation. My children were amazed, my husband stunned: homemade challah? Made by me? The non-baker? The exhausted mom who didn't have a moment to spare?

That was then.

A BRIEF HISTORY OF CHALLAH

Challah is not exactly new. Women have been making challah for thousands of years. Sarah, one of our matriarchs, baked her challah nearly four thousand years ago. What is this most marvelous of breads? The *Merriam-Webster Dictionary* defines challah as this: *egg-rich yeast-leavened bread that is usually braided or twisted before baking and is traditionally eaten by Jews on the Sabbath and holidays.*

Challah embodies both spiritual and physical elements. The root of the word challah is *chol*. Translated, *chol* means ordinary, secular. And in the process of making this dough, the ordinary becomes extraordinary, the secular becomes spiritual: historically, a piece of the dough—the challah—is separated and *elevated*, given to the priests in the Temple. The making and the eating of challah are not like the making and eating of any other bread or foodstuff: challah becomes a secular metaphor for manna from heaven, and how it is made reflects this elevated status. The process of making challah even includes saying a prayer before baking the dough and saying another prayer just before eating the baked challah.

I didn't know any of this when I started making challah; in fact, I didn't know any of it for years while I was making challah. It wasn't until several years ago—when I couldn't walk away from this activity, when it had become a part of me, when I realized that I was rearranging my Fridays to accommodate making challah—that I endeavored to learn its secrets, its history.

Making challah is a mitzvah, which is a commandment of Jewish law and a meritorious act. Completing a mitzvah, therefore, is much like completing a good deed. In the Jewish bible, there are over six hundred mitzvot (actually 613, but who's counting) designed to improve every aspect of our daily lives. We do these mitzvot all the time. Categorized and analyzed for our benefit, there are so many ways to do good. We can study them as individuals or as a community in order to learn how to behave in any circumstance. In the Torah, the Bible, we have at our disposal a literal guidebook on *how to be good*. In this crazy mixed-up world that is moving so fast, I greatly appreciate having an illuminated path.

The mitzvot are divided into many sections that detail how we should conduct ourselves in every aspect of our lives—from how to act in a family, to how to properly conduct business, to how we must help those less fortunate than ourselves. Making challah is mitzvah #385 (according to the *Sefer ha-Chinuch*, or the *Book of Education*).

Of all the mitzvot, there are three that are usually completed just by women, all three related to Shabbas. Therefore, I like to think of Shabbas through the lens of a feminist history. I practice two of these mitzvot: separation of the challah from the dough and lighting of the Shabbas candles. The third of these, practicing the laws of family purity, are mainly observed by Orthodox Jews, and I am not Orthodox.

Judaism has clearly defined roles for men and women, and although I don't agree with all of the rules that limit opportunities for either gender, I like how these three usually women-only mitzvot really do embody the role of women globally in Judaism. Whereas men in traditional Judaism study Torah, bringing the light down from above, it is the women who elevate this light, who take the mundane, the ordinary, the physical, and elevate it, make it extraordinary, make it spiritual. We women take a house and its contents and make it a home. When I've spoken to various rabbis about this concept, whether at the Jewish Family Experience—a Cleveland-area Jewish study center—or at Aish Los Angeles, I have been told that today's "real" Temple, the epicenter of our Jewish identity, is within the walls of each of our homes—homes that we create.

The true mitzvah of making challah occurs after the dough has been made and left to rise: the actual mitzvah occurs with the "separation of the dough," this small piece that one removes and prays over once the entire batch of dough rises. (Some challah bakers separate the dough once the ingredients are mixed and the dough is formed, but before it rises. I have never seen it done this way, and am in no rush to try it. I prefer to wait until the dough has risen.) Long ago, challah bakers gave this separated piece of dough to the *Kohenim*, the temple priests, to eat. Specifically, it is written in Numbers 15: 17-21: *"... It shall be that when you eat the bread of the land, you shall set aside a portion [of dough] for God."* I love that. I love that on a specific page in the Torah, at a specific spot in this guidebook for living, there lies the how and why of challah. It gets me every time; I can't believe that the Torah has an answer for everything. It always does. Even though there is no longer a Temple (the Second Temple was destroyed in 70 CE), even though there are no *Kohenim* waiting for their piece of dough, I still separate a piece of challah and say the blessing. This special moment of fulfilling a mitzvah connects me to our collective past and leads me toward our future.

It has made me believe. It has made me really ask the big questions, to look beyond what I learned in science class in school, theories of evolution and all that. It's made me think there is no such thing as coincidence. Things happen for a reason. If I wasn't convinced of this before, I most definitely am now.

I just recently learned that the separation of the challah is only mandated for dough that is suitable for actually making bread. I learned that I don't actually have to do this mitzvah because, technically, the amount of ingredients I usually use doesn't qualify me to perform the mitzvah. Truly, sometimes truth is stranger than fiction. *Suitable for making bread?* Oy, leave it to my forefathers to define it to such a level. Between the Torah itself and the Talmud, composed of the Mishnah (that would be the oral, spoken Torah) and the Gemara (that would be more description of the Mishnah plus the Tannaitic writings), there is a lot of room for interpretation! In fact, the Talmud contains more than 6,200 pages and includes many rabbinic interpretations and teachings on a variety of Jewish laws and customs. It is the basis of Jewish law. Sometimes I find this reassuring. I like having a roadmap; I like knowing why something is the way it is. At other times, I find it just overwhelming. How can I possibly learn it all? (I can't.)

Isn't all challah created equal? Isn't the making of all challah sanctified? Not according to the Talmudic interpretation.

To be precise, to be *halakhic* ("adj. description of laws and traditions that guide our religious practices and even some daily-life practices"), a minimum amount of flour must be used if one is to separate the challah from it. So that's it, then: it all comes down just to the flour, not the other ingredients. I usually fall a bit short. Well actually, a lot short: the only recipe that I've ever used, the one that I've come to think of as "My Recipe," calls for approximately four cups of flour—somewhere in the neighborhood of a pound. Halakhic law dictates that I use approximately *five pounds* of flour in order to be able to bless the separation of the challah. This number, by the way, was not pulled out of thin air; rather, it is found in the Talmud from a precise reading of the Torah.

Lesser amounts of dough are not halakhic, and therefore these amounts don't mandate separation of the challah with the subsequent blessing of the separated piece. Why? Because. Full stop. And there you have it. Six thousand two hundred pages of interpretation, and sometimes no better answer exists than *because it says so.* (The Talmud *says so* to me, and I *say so* to my children. If it's good enough for the Talmud, shouldn't it be good enough for me to *just say so?* Isn't that the right of all parents? Are we Talmud-like for our kids?) And isn't that just like life? Sometimes things just are. Kids' birthday parties usually start on time (well, at least that's what my father always said), taxes are due on April 15 every year, and you need five pounds of flour to be considered halakhic when making challah.

In hindsight, it's all rather obvious: I was not raised an observant Jew, so I didn't bother myself with laws like these. Actually, it's not that I didn't bother with the laws. I didn't even know that they existed in the first place. My family rarely ate challah. Occasionally, we bought one at the kosher grocery store on Taylor Road. That store intimidated me, made me think of women congregating in the shtetl, speaking a language I didn't speak, bartering and jostling for unfamiliar foods in a tight space filled with unfamiliar smells. I still get a little overwhelmed in kosher grocery stores, though I seek them out, drawn to them like a magnet. I can and do find myself wandering up and down all the aisles, reading the labels, wondering, *Who eats this food? How do they prepare it? What does this food say about them?*

What does it say that I did not grow up eating challah? We walked a fine line years ago, my family. In a race to fulfill the American Dream, to keep movin' on up, my grandfather ran from his Judaism as fast as his 5-foot-7-inch frame could carry him. My father continued that tradition. Simply, we were cultural Jews who liked matzo ball soup, lox and bagels, and the Brooklyn Dodgers. I doubt my father knew of any of Judaism's rich history or traditions. My parents ran, and they ran fast. They ran from those who told them which part of the neighborhood they could live in. They ran from the mean kids who pulled anti-Semitic pranks, including a dead bird left one day in my father's mailbox when he was a boy. They ran toward new traditions, gathering to open stocking stuffers before digging into a Christmas breakfast feast, followed by opening presents under the tree. I brought that beautiful stocking, rich creams and whites with sequins, the one my mom sewed for me as a child, here to Los Angeles with me. It has made each move of mine, tucked quietly in a plastic storage bin. I can't part with it. I won't.

Growing up, my family practiced what is known as Reform Judaism. Much of Judaism is divided into Reform, Conservative, Orthodox, and even Reconstructionist—labels I have always found divisive and disruptive. As I saw it then, Orthodox Jews followed all the mitzvot to the letter of the law, the Reform got to pick and choose what worked for them and the Conservative fell somewhere in between. I realize now that the distinctions are more nuanced, especially as I learn more about the mitzvot and their significance. The more I learn, the more I find myself adhering to more mitzvot. After all, action leads to belief. The pieces of the puzzle come together, and I take an easier breath.

My father's family assimilated when they emigrated from Eastern Europe to America in the mid- to late 1800s. My mother's family emigrated from Europe, as well, and once settled in America, went so far as to ultimately choose Quakerism over Judaism. By the time my parents came of age, several generations into life in America, their families had assimilated and identified as Reform Jews. My father did not have a bar mitzvah, and once married, my parents did not keep an observant home. In turn, I didn't have a bat mitzvah when I turned thirteen, and as a result, I didn't know many of the prayers, the rituals, or associated practices until much later, when I no longer lived at home. I didn't know the intricacies of Shabbas, about the mitzvot of lighting the candles and the making and eating of challah. Naturally, I knew about mitzvot in general, knew that to do a good deed constituted a mitzvah. I knew the classic story about a pomegranate: on Rosh Hashanah, we always have decorative pomegranates on the table and eat pomegranate seeds, as it was said that each pomegranate contains 613 seeds, each one representing a mitzvah. That's about all that I knew.

I still pick and choose pieces and parts of Judaism, though as I get older, I choose to pick more. Making challah each Friday is but one more example. Although the Torah originally mandated that the mitzvah of making challah had been performed in *Eretz Yisroel* (that's in Israel, for you and me) so that a piece of the bread could be given to the priests at the Temple, we also continue this mitzvah outside of Israel today, in the Diaspora (everywhere Jews live but in Israel), so we don't forget. Doing one thing to remind us to remember another thing. I believe this practice connects me to women *everywhere,* then and there, here and now. Our matriarch Sarah performed this mitzvah, and a rebbetzin (wife of a rabbi) here in Los Angeles I know today performs this mitzvah. I have friends all over Los Angeles, Cleveland, and New York who perform this mitzvah. You bet I'm going to say the blessing and keep making challah—five pounds of flour or not.

MAKING THE CHALLAH

The Journey

⁓∞⁓

The following steps to the challah recipe are my journey for how I began to find my own wellness. Through these, I learned the lessons of slowing down, of keeping it simple, and of reconnecting to other women. I learned something so simple and yet so profound: I could take the time to bake bread once a week, every week. In the midst of being a physician and a wife and a mother and so much more, I could take a little time to recalibrate myself. The following steps showed me the way.

Step One:

Finding Time on Fridays

Challah is served Friday night for Shabbas dinner. I make challah, therefore, on Fridays so that it is fresh for that night. I could make it earlier in the week, or even further in advance, and freeze it. I don't. I like it fresh, preferably just warm out of the oven. Actually, I am a little afraid to vary my routine. This way works, and works well. What if it doesn't taste as good if I make it a day early? What if it doesn't defrost well if I make it several days earlier? Is it okay for it to taste different? Must it always be the same?

One of these days, I'm just going to take the risk. Maybe I'll make it on a Tuesday and see what happens. It's not like I'm mixing a formula in a science laboratory; it's not like I'm solving the Arab-Israeli conflict. It's just bread.

Unless we are away, I have made challah almost every Friday since that first Friday ten years ago and counting. *Food is medicine.* I believe this. I teach this. I practice this, as a physician, writer, and mother. Usually, I mean this to be in the context of *eating* food. Eat a balanced diet with minimal processed foods and with minimal ingredients such as trans fats and high fructose corn syrup. I prefer to prescribe eating a diet rich in nutrients and whole foods, rather than popping pills. It's more logical to me, and fortunately, more and more supported in the medical literature.

Since I began this journey, I've learned that *making* food can be medicinal in its own right; and for me, that's making challah.

It can be for you, too.

What originally began as my own experiment developed into something beyond me, larger, out of my control. My children began to depend on this homemade challah every Friday. And so did their cousins and their friends, even my mom and my mother-in-law. Eventually, my friends wanted to learn how to make their own challah, too. We started our own little revolution in our own little corner of the world, one challah at a time.

First I was making challah. And then Dana was making it. And Hannah. And Marne. And Pamela. And Laura. And Sarah. And, and, and. The texts and emails fly back and forth on Fridays. What to do if the yeast doesn't proof. How to fold in chocolate chips or apple pieces. Can the dough be made on Thursday night instead of Friday? Can a mixer stand in for kneading by hand? And then the beautiful pictures begin to appear in my inbox. Single braids, two challahs, round challahs. Gorgeous bread made by gorgeous women, who have all taken a moment to stop and breathe, who are all just a little bit more at peace this week, or at least this Friday morning.

And *when* do you just stop and make challah? It's not always easy squeezing this mitzvah into a busy Friday. If I know that I won't be able to set aside enough time during the day, sometimes I set my alarm clock and wake extra early that morning, before sunrise, to make the dough. I really love that time of morning anyway, the sunlight just contemplating peeking through the trees while I tiptoe around the kitchen, trying not to wake any of our children while I get out ingredients, warm up the water. If I am really fortunate, I get to glimpse the moon just before it descends for the day.

Sometimes I make the dough late in the day on Friday, just before our guests arrive for Shabbas dinner. And although that is the most stressful time of the day for me to make the dough—I worry that it won't be done on time—the bread is at its best when it's just plucked warm from the oven. More and more, I just fit making the dough into my schedule for the day and if it rises for one hour or an hour and a half, so be it. Through making dough, I have learned to take things more in stride, as they happen.

I make challah almost every Friday. Even if we are going to another friend's home for Shabbas dinner and they will have their own challah, I still make it. Good habits are just as hard to break as bad habits. Rarely, though, it does happen that I just can't figure out how to make the time—although it did happen last Friday.

I woke up in a panic. The light on my small alarm clock showed 4:28 a.m. My mother was in town for a visit, asleep downstairs next to the kitchen. I couldn't have made the dough then if I had wanted to—I might have awakened her. (Another commandment: honor your parents. I didn't even know that I was performing a mitzvah, but how lovely to find a silver lining to counterbalance the horror of being awake at that ungodly hour.) Yet I felt obligated to make challah for her. How could I do all that I had to do that day and still find the time to make the dough? I watched the clock until the sun rose. A few hours later, when I thought it acceptable to sneak into the kitchen, coffee in hand, headache held in check, I peeked into the freezer just before 7 a.m., ever so grateful to see a lone homemade frozen challah tucked neatly away on a shelf, behind the frozen premade waffles. I vowed to add an eleventh commandment then and there: there shall *always* be a frozen challah in the freezer. Just in case.

So now I often double the recipe, and I love all the reasons why: more for us for dinner, or more to bring if we are going to a friend's for Shabbas dinner, or more for leftovers for a large batch of French toast Saturday morning. It also makes for great sandwich bread during the week for school lunches, so much easier to slice when still slightly frozen. But since yeast still intimidates me, when I make two batches, I do so separately. I am too afraid to double the yeast. What will happen? The fear of the unknown results in double the amount of dirty bowls and baking sheets. Wouldn't it just be easier to double the recipe in *one* bowl, with twice as much yeast? Maybe for some women, but not for me. The goal, remember, is to be present. Not to be stressed out.

Finding Connections

When I had my clinical practice, one of my favorite parts of examining a patient occurred when I auscultated her heart, when I just listened to her heartbeat. My left hand was on the chest piece of the stethoscope, pressed to her chest; my right hand was up on her shoulder, or perhaps resting on her upper back. I listened for that rhythmic lub-dub. And I listened for any irregularities, perhaps a murmur or a click. But I also listened for myself. For a moment, to just be. To hear a heartbeat, to hear a reminder of life—to just pause for a few ticks. This quick moment of listening to a patient's heartbeat—alone, in my own little world, with my own thoughts—never failed to ground me, to connect me to the women around me.

And making challah has become about connection for me. I now often bake with other women. We bake in my kitchen; we bake in theirs. Doesn't matter. What matters is that we are together, sharing an experience that women have shared together for nearly four thousand years.

I started making challah with other women when we moved to Los Angeles. Having made this bread week after week already for almost five years, I felt comfortable with the recipe, with my routine. I knew how to make it; it was time to share. Originally, I just had friends over who expressed an interest, women who had eaten the challah at our home and wanted to try making it themselves. They come on Fridays, usually in the mornings. Depending on whether they will let the dough rise at my home or whether they will take the dough to rise at their home, I suggest that they bring either a bowl or a baking sheet. I like to provide everything else. I like to set up the *mise en place* for them.

All good things change. Now I don't just have friends over. Now, sometimes, strangers come over to bake, too. Occasionally I get a call about someone who wants to learn how to make challah, even though I don't know her personally.

And we make challah together. Mixing ingredients, spending time in close proximity, saying blessings—these actions are intimate and personal, and quickly we come together over the bowls of dough. New friends or old friends, we've spoken of cancer diagnoses; we've spoken of classmates of our children wrestling with suicide and addiction. We've spoken of being caught between our parents and our children. We've spoken about our changing bodies and of the men in our lives. And all the while, we keep stirring the ingredients, we keep kneading the dough.

On those Friday nights, on the west side of LA, I know now that more of my friends share challah together and more of my friends think about Shabbas. And that makes the clinician in me—the teacher—*happy, fulfilled.*

Making your own challah on Fridays gets addictive. Just ask my friend Laura. She tries to make her own challah every week, too. If we're lucky and we can coordinate our schedules, we even try to make it together. How hard can this be? We're practically next-door neighbors. Unfortunately, we don't have the opportunity to make it together too frequently, but often check in with each other to see how this week's batch turned out. When my phone rang several Fridays ago, just before I planned to light the Shabbas candles, and I saw her name pop up on the caller ID, I assumed that's why she was calling.

"You know Stephanie, right?" she asked. Of course I know Stephanie. I've made challah with Stephanie; and I always bring her my challah when I go to her home. "Yes," I told Laura, "I know Stephanie."

"Well," Laura went on, "I met her today at Vicente Foods.

Buying challah. I know, right, I shouldn't have been buying challah, but I ran out of time and the only place I'll buy it is there. So there I was, buying challah next to your friend, who was also buying challah. And somehow we both mentioned that we don't usually buy challah, but here we were. And I said that I usually make it with my friend Beth. And she said, Oh, you mean Beth Ricanati? *I* make challah with her, too."

We have sparked our own little revolution, in our own little corner of the world. I love that these two former New Yorkers were standing in the cramped bakery aisle of that grocery store, almost apologetic that they were buying challah instead of making their own. I love that they were even considering having challah at all on that Friday night. This bread grounds us, brings us together, in ways I could never have imagined.

Step Two:

Gather Your Ingredients

2¼ teaspoons loose yeast + 1 teaspoon sugar + 1 cup very warm water (almost too warm, but not hot!), 2 eggs, 2 teaspoons salt, ¼ cup sugar, ⅓ cup oil, 4 plus cups flour

Making challah does not equate to an exercise in curing cancer, or some other Herculean task. Making challah involves simply mixing six ingredients in a bowl. I've learned, though, that it matters which flour you use, which eggs, which sugar, which salt, which oil and which yeast. The better the ingredient, the better the end product. I've learned a similar lesson when I cook with wine, but that's another story.

Oil: Use Canola

The recipe that I originally used listed "vegetable oil" for the oil. I didn't question the directions; I just understood that to mean canola oil. Why? Simple: canola oil usually sits on a shelf in my pantry, and so of course, it sat there that day and I reached for it. I didn't think too much about oil then. I just made the bread, liked making the bread, and stuck with the canola oil. What started out perhaps accidently became a realization: canola is a neutral oil. As such, it doesn't distract from the other ingredients. Canola oil therefore works perfectly for this challah-making job.

I actually never knew what might happen if I strayed from using this simple, neutral canola oil until one wintry day just last year. I had gone one Friday morning to my friend Marne's house to make challah with her. Standing on her front stoop, just about to ring her doorbell, ingredients in hand, I realized that all good planning aside, I had forgotten the oil. No big deal—or so I thought. It's not as though we would need very much. Just ⅓ cup. Who doesn't have a little canola oil around?

A bad assumption—which reminded me of something my sister told me one day when she came home from her summer job at the local newspaper and shared with me a funny expression that her boss, an editor there, had told her. I was still in junior high, a time when a swear word still held some sway. Don't *ass*ume, she told me. It will make an *ass* out of "u" and an *ass* out of "me." Still gets me. So there I stood, so many years later, in Marne's kitchen, assuming that she'd have canola oil.

She didn't. She had lots of olive oil, both straight up olive oil and extra virgin olive oil, but using olive oil to make challah didn't feel right. Mixing the two seemed almost sacrilegious. Olive oil was not for bread making. I used olive oil for whisking into salad dressing, for sauté-ing and marinating. We kept digging through her pantry, and there, tucked behind a few bottles in her cupboard, Marne unearthed a 50/50 blended oil: canola with olive oil. "That might work," she said, and I agreed.

We proceeded to make the dough, but the olive oil dough *felt* different than our usual challah dough. The consistency was not what I had become accustomed to. Not a bad feeling, necessarily, just different. And worse, it had a strong aroma. I had never smelled olive-y challah before, and I didn't like it, wasn't used to it. It smelled fruity. It smelled misplaced. I hadn't realized that I had come to like the aroma of my challah—or more specifically, the *lack* of any particular aroma. What I liked smelled like freshly baked bread, pure and simple, and that turned out to be more important than I knew. Olive-oil challah did not deliver the correct sensory experience for me. The bread we made that day was soft and golden, but I considered it inferior to canola-oil challah.

Flash-forward to dinner. I served the olive oil challah and even though it tasted slightly different, everyone ate it just as quickly as usual, no comments from the peanut gallery. But I *knew*. And it bothered me. And then I understood the problem: it wasn't really about the olive oil. The problem lay in that I had knowingly taken a shortcut. I should have taken the extra ten minutes to stop at the local grocery store and purchase more canola oil before I rang Marne's doorbell, but in my rush that morning, I had compromised, and it showed.

We rush all the time, we take shortcuts all the time. *What are we doing with those extra minutes that we save?* I should have taken a moment, procured the ingredients that I preferred to work with, done it right. You know, Boy Scouts and all that: I should've been prepared. It makes life so much easier, and challah so much tastier.

Although I know intellectually it's not as simple as using this oil or that oil when I make challah, I also know that I have the power to improve the odds. Not with fancy diets, not with crazy food restrictions, not with a medicine cabinet full of the latest supplements. Just with good, smart food choices. *Food is medicine.* Don't forget it. Perhaps Wendell Berry said it best: "People are fed by the food industry, which pays no attention to health, and are treated by the health industry, which pays no attention to food." What I know to be true: pay attention to what you eat. Pay attention to what you choose to put in your mouth. You're not going to put tomato juice in your car's gas tank and expect to drive off into the sunset, so why put something unhealthy, processed or chemical-based in your body and expect to feel good, to be healthy?

Pay attention. You can, and you should. It's your body.

I keep trying.

I should take a moment to comment on what can happen when you change up the ingredients because you are seduced by trends. This happened to my friend Pamela. She started using my recipe this past summer to make challah and she modified it from the start by using coconut oil. Coconut oil is the rage right now here in Southern California.

Since moving to California, I have seen coconut oil—and coconut cooking spray and coconut-based sugar, in fact a plethora of coconut-based foods—in many a friend's kitchen, on the shelves at stores like Whole Foods and Trader Joe's, and now in more mainstream grocery stores as well. It's tasty in Asian foods, in curry, and even in some of my go-to recipes that I am trying to make nondairy, such as in my favorite pancake recipe or in my banana chocolate chip bread recipe.

But as my friend learned that Friday afternoon, coconut oil does not easily substitute for canola oil in challah. Both the texture and the taste of Pamela's challah were off, and she knew it. Many of us have eaten challah before, and we have a preconceived idea of what it should taste and look like. And while we often embrace change, change is not usually so welcome when it comes to the taste of challah. Pamela has since returned to making challah with canola oil. Recently, just before a Friday night dinner of hers, she texted me a picture of her beautiful challah and I could almost taste it: two perfectly golden braided loaves.

Since moving to California, I have started to cook more, and have learned more about the nuances of various cooking oils. So many oils, so little time. There sits the canola oil on the shelf. And vegetable oil. And olive oil. And now coconut oil. Several dozen oils at any given grocery store, hundreds if you get into the specialty shops and start thinking about source and process. But in sticking with canola oil, I keep it simple.

For me, for my challah, for my life now, simplicity reigns. Just the basics, ma'am. Often, at the grocery store, I'll buy whatever canola oil is on the shelf. This neutral oil allows me to focus on the end product, the challah. The gift to myself: I am just doing it, just baking the bread. Making bread should be simple. If not, I risk a Californian Sisyphean moment, endlessly searching for the perfect oil. Of course, exactly what that perfect oil may be could always change. I suppose today it would be organic, non-GMO canola oil, locally sourced, in a recyclable glass (or at least BPA-free) container. But some days, I just can't have it all.

SIDEBAR: Doesn't Oil Make You Fat?

Not all oil is created equal. Some oils are good for you (olive oil, for example), and some oils aren't as good for you (palm oil, for example). Some oils contain saturated fats and some contain unsaturated fats. Fortunately, canola oil contains a mono-unsaturated fat—fats that can help to lower LDL, the "bad" cholesterol, and in turn lower your risk for heart disease. (I know, I've said it before, but lowering your risk of heart disease is a bit of an obsession with me.) Canola oil is also loaded with omega-3 and omega-6 fatty acids. We need these fatty acids because our bodies can't make them on their own. We need them because the research continues to show just how much our heart and brain health rely on these beneficial omega acids.

I don't like "flavored" challah, and thus oils such as coconut, olive, and avocado don't work for me when making challah. And I understand that conventionally processed canola oil has its downsides, especially in regards to oxidized fats and trans fats. Since I only use it occasionally—in fact, primarily just on Fridays when I make challah—and since I seek out organic, cold-pressed canola oils that have less oxidized and trans fats, I feel okay about this choice.

I care a lot about both heart health and brain health. I don't want dementia: my grandfather and father had dementia. I don't want heart disease: my other grandfather had a heart attack. I want to grow old and someday let my hair grow gray. I want to hold my grandchildren in my arms and bake challah with them as they grow up. I want to dance with my husband when we are too old to dance.

Flour: Get All-Purpose, King Arthur if you can find it

Flour was the first ingredient that I consciously started to tweak once I felt comfortable making the dough. The recipe called for four cups of flour. Originally, I assumed that meant white flour. However, as a physician and a mother trying to feed her children healthy food, I thought I should do the "right" thing: I thought that I needed to up the whole-grain quotient.

I began to try various ratios of whole wheat to white flour—two to one, two to two, two to four. No matter how many different permutations I experimented with, I could never get a worthwhile product. Finally, after many attempts, I decided that *Hashem* (Hebrew word for God) would approve of my efforts to make challah regardless of the white flour, and I let it go at that. I believe that *perfect* equals the enemy of the good. Once I was aware of that, I could take a different approach.

And poor-tasting challah is just that. Poor. My challah made with whole grains tasted dry. It tasted leaden. It did not taste good. It was not the type of bread that I wanted to serve my family on Shabbas.

I went back to using white flour, just pure, unadulterated white flour—and the challah remained sublime. Everyone breathed a sigh of relief. Again, all things are in balance. And white flour once a week in my challah recipe was once again okay. *Keep it simple,* I reminded myself. Just keep it simple.

I use AP (all-purpose) flour, by the way, because it's easy—one flour, many purposes. I'm not interested making anything more complicated than necessary—even something as simple as making bread. Actually, I didn't even know that other flours existed, such as bread flour and cake flour. I didn't know how they differed from AP flour and if that difference would affect my challah.

I have learned that bread flour has greater protein content in it than AP flour. This is relevant for its purpose: to make great bread. The higher protein content helps with gluten development, which can result in a denser, more chewy loaf. The wheat used in bread flour consists of high-gluten, hard wheat. The flour in cake flour consists of high-starch, soft wheat. AP flour falls in the middle. It is literally *all-purpose*, the workhorse of flours.

SIDEBAR:

What's the deal with the gluten-free craze?

First, let's start by defining gluten. Simply, gluten is a protein found in many types of grains. Some people either have a disease like celiac, or some have gluten intolerance and should not ingest gluten. Most scientists agree that overall this is quite a small percentage of the population. However, there has been much written today about a gluten-free diet. In a multibillion-dollar diet industry, there is always something new, and currently, gluten-free occupies this vaunted status.

However, gluten is okay for most of us. Actually, in researching gluten for this book, I learned that gluten doesn't even have any special nutritional benefits itself. Rather, it's what's in the grains themselves that is so important. Avoiding grains means avoiding many wonderful nutrients —including fiber, which most women do not get enough of in their diets. We women need twenty-five grams of fiber daily. That's really hard to do once you drop the whole grains out of the equation.

Food is medicine. And whole grains are part of that prescription. The 2010 Dietary Guidelines for Americans recommend that a whopping 50 percent of all your carbohydrates come from whole-grain products—so important because these nutrients can modify your risk of diseases such as heart disease, cancer, and diabetes.

Recently, at the insistence of a friend with whom I bake challah, I substituted King Arthur's flour for my go-to white flour. I was not convinced that swapping flours would make much of a difference. Flour is flour. Except when it's not. I found the requisite bag of King Arthur's at the second grocery store that I tried, tucked in between the organic flour that I usually bought, and the store brand. When I got it home and opened the bag, I dipped a hand in, feeling the soft, silken texture, almost weightless. The dough made with this new flour was fun to knead; and the best part was that everyone noticed something different with the challah that night. My kids asked what I had done this time. My husband held his piece up to the light, examining it closely, trying to understand what had changed this week, what was new, what was different.

I love to run my hands through handfuls of flour now. It's a sensual, decadent experience, like touching my normally curly hair when I've had it blown out straight. Absentmindedly, I constantly run my fingers through them both. They're just so *damn* soft.

King Arthur Flour has been around for a long time—since 1790, to be exact. That's a long time to perfect something. And they have perfected more than just something, more than just flour. This company takes social responsibility to a new level, respecting their product (the flour itself), their company (their countless employees), and their community (the environmental footprint they are leaving; funding local organizations in their community). I like using a product from such an inspirational company for such an elevated purpose.

SIDEBAR: A Word About White Bread

During the course of writing this book, people often surprised me with the following query: "You're making challah, okay. But white bread . . . isn't bread bad for you? You're a DOCTOR. You should know better!" After making over one thousand challahs, I believe the answer is no, challah is not bad for you. Here's why: because challah provides both physical and spiritual nourishment.

Physical Nourishment:
My challah recipe has six ingredients in it. That's it. My challah is not filled with chemicals and additives and an abundance of ingredients that I can't pronounce. Six ingredients that are easy to pronounce. Similarly, good bread, regardless of the type—white bread or whole wheat bread, for example—is filled with good ingredients. Any bread with just a few simple ingredients that you can pronounce will probably taste good and have something nutritious in it for you.

"But white bread does not have all of those healthy whole grains," some persisted. "White bread is just empty carbs."

This complaint has some merit. Certainly many of us know by now that increasing whole grains in our diets may reduce our risk of so many diseases. Thus, I usually prescribe brown grains instead of white grains: brown rice, whole wheat breads and pasta, quinoa, farro, and spelt. While white grains have been stripped of many of their beneficial nutrients, their whole grain counterparts are full of complex carbohydrates, vitamins and minerals— all good things we need to stay healthy.

After all, food is powerful medicine: foods can turn on and off genes in our body. This in turn can help to promote disease or actually help to stave off disease. That's amazing. Just think: the broccoli that you cook tonight for dinner might actually help to prevent cancer.

With that said, I make challah with white flour, and using this white flour does not keep me up at night. Why? Because using white flour is a choice I make on Fridays; it is not a food group for me. Because I believe that to be healthy, truly healthy, balance is the way to go. Balance in the foods I eat; balance in the amount of exercise that I get; balance in all that I do. I strive for this— though I don't always attain it. Sometimes, like on Halloween, I have too many mini Snickers candy bars. Sometimes, when I am trying to meet a deadline, I don't make time to exercise. Sometimes, when my husband travels for business, I stay up until the early morning hours reading and don't get enough sleep. Sometimes, I heat up pizza for my kids instead of making a homemade dinner. When I use white flour to make my challah, I remind myself of the importance of balance. Making challah is my weekly reinforcement to go with the flow a bit more.

Spiritual Nourishment:
When Moses and the Israelites wandered in the desert for forty years, they found sustenance in manna that came down from above. Each day, they gathered enough manna for that day. On Shabbas, though, they gathered double the amount of manna because the following day was a day of rest. No manna gathering on the Sabbath.

To honor this intent of a day of rest on Shabbas, I make at least two loaves of challah each week.

Just before dinner, I place these two loaves on a platter, covering them. Before we eat dinner, we will say a blessing over them. Manna from heaven. Yes, it's white bread. But this challah that I make is sacred bread. This is special bread, not bread in general. This is bread that sustains us, bread that nurtures us.

Yeast: Buy Fleischmann's at the store or your favorite kind in bulk (I like Red Star)

Bread is bread because of the yeast. Otherwise, it's just a flat cracker. This yeast is the magic ingredient—the essential ingredient—to beautiful bread, bread that is fluffy and elastic. True bakers believe that bread made with yeast yields bread with a better crumb—a fancy way of saying that the crust is better, that it holds its shape better, that it's just plain *better*.

I remember all too well that first day in the baking aisle so long ago, standing there looking at all of the variations of yeast, the different types—active dry yeast versus instant dry yeast versus bread machine yeast (who knew?) versus cake yeast. I felt stranded, trapped in a place I didn't understand. Fortunately, an earnest young store employee took pity on me in my frazzled state. He ascertained the purpose for the yeast, then steered me to the individual packets of Fleischmann's—those little red packets, sitting pretty just above eye level in the baking aisle. I had most likely walked past the open boxes that contained the individual packets hundreds, if not thousands, of times, never even noticing them, as they sat patiently waiting for me to discover them.

Several years later, Hillary introduced me to bulk yeast. Hillary makes gorgeous challahs—chocolate, cinnamon, apple, even dusted with vanilla sugar—that she delivers wrapped lovingly in cellophane and tied with a beautiful ribbon. Her tip one day to buy yeast in bulk abated my frustration with purchasing yeast. I no longer needed to worry if I had enough packets on hand, if they were still good to use. I no longer needed to worry about them disappearing into the abyss of one of my cupboards. Their tiny size had made them easy to lose sight of on the shelf.

Though I still don't know everything about the different yeasts, I do know that active dry yeast works for me and for the challah that I make. I buy the bulk packet of Red Star Active Dry Yeast from Amazon. Vacuum-packed packages of bulk yeast arrive at my front door as if delivered by a modern-day stork. I like the look of the bulk yeast, the feel of it. I like that when I remember to order the yeast, it arrives in just a few days. No delay is incurred; my challah-making continues. I like that it is cheaper than the individual packets. And I like that this yeast is certified kosher pareve. I simply order, and then don't worry for another year.

Today, this loose yeast can be refrigerated or frozen, which extends its shelf life, often for as long as two years (though I've never tested the two-year mark). When my vacuum-sealed package of yeast arrives, I decant the contents of the package into a Tupperware container and store it in the refrigerator. Magically, this amount lasts for exactly one year. It doesn't matter how many challahs I make (and I made eight challahs three months ago for my nephew's bar mitzvah; only seven made it on the flight between LA and Portland—alas, we all couldn't resist getting an early start nibbling, the smell throughout our house that morning was just too much). This amount of yeast lasts one year, every year, from November to November. I don't know how or why, but the container of yeast connects itself to the calendar.

As I use up the yeast, I switch to smaller and smaller containers. And I always have too much. The recipe calls for 2¼ teaspoons, and my Amazon shipment is of the one-size variety. I could sustain a small community with that little vacuum-sealed package. I can't begin to use it all. Inevitably, I end up sharing small containers with friends as they learn how to bake their own challah.

Warm Water: Just shy of too hot to touch

Sometimes, of course, it's not just about what kind of yeast to purchase. Often it's about how to bring yeast to life with warm water and sugar. There's something about yeast that remains unknown, forbidden, invisible, magic. The word *proof* is so apt: kick-starting the yeast, getting ready to bake with it, is much like solving a mathematical *proof.* Identical word, similar meaning to me. I like the symmetry.

Sometimes the water temperature feels too hot for the yeast; sometimes I forget the teaspoon of sugar and nothing happens. The yeast just sits there, useless. It's not a good feeling. The water must be only warm.

So what exactly defines warm water? Is it warm to my touch; is it too hot to my touch? Will I need a thermometer to measure the water temperature? I was not so sure when I first started making challah. Therefore, without too much forethought, I chose the path of least resistance: I used my own tap water just at the moment when it felt almost too hot to touch. And since the yeast and sugar mixture ultimately bubbled as per instructed, I assumed that this temperature qualified as "warm."

The house that I first made challah in dated to the 1920s, replete with an old water heater that had been readjusted by our handyman. I didn't want our young children scalding themselves with hot bath water. Little did I know that an ancillary benefit to my safety precaution resulted in the perfect temperature for "warm water" to proof yeast. We recently readjusted the water in our current house; I have to pay closer attention to the water temperature when I proof the yeast for the next few weeks, until I again just intuitively know what the right temperature is, how long I must heat up the water. I almost threw out the yeast mixture yesterday. I had actually turned the temperature down to get what I thought was the right temperature, and then while I went about making the dough, the yeast mixture did its thing. Only it looked different than usual. Same bubbles, but the water remained murky. I couldn't actually start over, though. I had to finish making the dough and leave the house right then. I worried all afternoon; I worried until one of my son's friends exclaimed loudly as he opened the front door later that afternoon: "Is it only me, or does it really smell *marvelous* in here?" Out of the mouths of babes, or in this case, a fourteen-year-old young man. Why is it that a compliment from a friend of one of my children has the power to change everything? The bread would be okay. That boy had guaranteed that. And it was, a few hours later. Seven children at the table, a smattering of adults, and just challah crumbs to sweep up this morning.

Curiosity ultimately led me to look up the ideal temperature for proofing yeast. Not that I wanted to actually measure the temperature of the water with a thermometer; I just wanted to know. I learned that yeast is happiest somewhere between 75° and 80°. Thus, the yeast-water-sugar mixture should be warm, but not too warm, to the touch. Get it right, and the magic happens.

Sugar: Buy plain old white sugar

Have you stood in the baking aisle of your grocery store recently, trying to decide which sugar to purchase? It's utterly overwhelming. There is pure cane sugar—white sugar, usually fine or extra fine. There is confectioner's sugar, granulated white sugar, ground to a smooth powder that also contains a bit of cornstarch to keep it from caking. There is brown sugar—both light brown sugar and dark brown sugar. Don't be confused, however: the darker brown sugar has more molasses flavor and a richer color. Muscovado and demerara are brown sugars, especially popular in England, although I have recently seen demerara sugar mentioned more frequently in baking recipes that have crossed my desk. There is also turbinado (turban-*what?*) sugar, a raw sugar, in the brown sugar family. At last count at my favorite local grocery store, there were way too many different kinds of sugar. They all have different tastes, act differently when used for baking, and in fact have specific purposes for food preparations by those in the know. That would not be me.

All those years ago, standing in the baking aisle of my local grocery, I just wanted to make challah. The recipe called for "sugar." Not knowing the abundant vagaries of sugar, I just chose plain white sugar. Later on, as I started purchasing more organic foods, I switched the sugar to organic as well. Still, my mantra remained the same: keep it simple, and just stick to plain organic cane sugar for making challah. When serving it, I occasionally add honey.

SIDEBAR: Isn't Sugar Bad for Us?

Should we be worried about too much sugar? Unequivocally yes. We consume too much. Period. And excess sugar in our diets has been implicated in so many diseases. Diseases that you either have or that someone you know has. Alas, even the most well-intentioned of us sometimes err, myself included. I was a wellness physician running a lifestyle modification program and I know just how much sugar is too much. I also know that the amount of sugar in one batch of challah that I make only once a week is just fine. What I sometimes forget is the amount of sugar in everything else. It should be as simple as reading the label on the back of the food package.

For sugar, a serving should be less than four grams. So much for those little cartons of organic chocolate milk I used to give my kids when they were young: twenty-two grams of sugar in one carton. Ouch.

But what I see as too much, others see as just fine: cue the Great Chocolate Milk debacle of 2011. We had lived in Santa Monica for a little less than a year when the Los Angeles Unified School District (the second largest school district in the nation) banned chocolate milk from their school lunch program. Marvelous—and about time, or so I and some other parents and students in our school district thought. We'll just ask our own local school board to do the same. It seemed so logical, so obvious. And yet, after a contentious run-in with the school board, we failed in our efforts. Chocolate milk, loaded with sugar and other nonessential—and definitely unhealthy— ingredients, stayed on the menu. And once again I learned a very important lesson: just because I believe something to be true, it doesn't mean that others agree with me.

I have taught our children that water and plain, unflavored milk are healthier options than flavored milk. I have recommended to them that they stay away from the chocolate milk served at school. However, I sometimes put honey on the table to go with the challah. And I sometimes dip my piece of challah in that pot of honey. After all, balance, in all things, is what I should strive for.

Eggs: Get farmer's market eggs if you can

Eggs help bind the challah dough, acting as the requisite glue. My recipe calls for two eggs. But should they be big eggs, small eggs, brown eggs, white eggs, cage-free eggs, organic eggs? At first, I did not give it much thought. I just grabbed whatever eggs I had in the refrigerator on any given Friday. Then we moved across the country to Southern California. Here, I quickly discovered that not all eggs are created equal.

I started to go to the farmer's market each week in my newly adopted state, which I have come to learn provides much of our nation's food. Previously, I did not realize this. Rather, I didn't often think about where our food actually came *from*. I had been lulled into believing that lettuce came in a presealed bag on a cooled shelf at the grocery store, that carrots naturally grew in to those tiny little bite-size pieces, that cucumbers had no taste, just a crunchy sensation.

The breadbasket for our country is in area called the Central Valley, which is, in fact, in the center of California. This vast area, approximately 22,500 square miles in scope, produces enormous quantities of food for our nation, and beyond—over two hundred different crops. The harvest includes foods that we eat every day, or should eat: fruits and vegetables, eggs and nuts and meat. It's one thing to purchase these foods in a grocery store. It's quite another to be able to purchase them at a farmer's market, fresh, in season. Local. Sometimes organic. Maybe even from the farmer herself. A farmer's market filled with almost all the fruits and vegetables that we eat, not just a few of them. I get to dip my hand into a treasure chest each week and come up a winner. And the eggs! I could rhapsodize all day about farmer's market eggs. They look different to me—earthy and brown, with deep golden yolks. These new yolks were almost burnt orange in color, reminding me of saffron. Actually, it is a yellow so deep, it's almost like the marigolds we planted with my mom in the vegetable garden as children to keep out the slugs. I liked to arrange the marigolds in colorful patterns around the tomato plants, usually in a crisscross riot of color, the yellows and oranges a sharp contrast to the brown dirt and green leaves.

And these eggs certainly taste different to me. They alter the foods they are added to. My challah now always looks golden; it looks luxurious. This seems appropriate, as we lift the bread up and say a prayer before we eat it. It should be golden, royal almost. It should be special.

Eggs exemplify how food is influenced by our surroundings, our environment. They are transformed by their climate, their local culture. Just like us. Each week, at the farmer's market, I purchase eighteen eggs. I can choose brown or white eggs, both in gray compostable containers. I always choose the brown ones; I'm not sure why, other than it feels more authentic. They *look* more authentic. If my Shabbas table will be larger this week, or I am making extra challah for friends, then I purchase two eighteen-egg cartons. When all else fails, the extra eggs make for great scrambled eggs, or perhaps a frittata if I have leftover vegetables, as well.

"Fresh farm eggs here. Get your farm fresh eggs *h-e-e-e-re*," the lovely Hispanic woman exhorts loudly each week. I always stop at her table. Her sign, written in lopsided English on an oblong piece of cardboard, tacked up against her table, promises eggs from "happy chickens." How can I resist a happy chicken?

I can't.

I try to always have correct change for her. If she can provide for happy chickens, raised on a farm just north of Los Angeles, then I believe that having exact change is the only appropriate course of action.

Buying these eggs directly, face-to-face, makes me feel like part of a community. And in a new community, far away from my "roots," I appreciate this. I have always liked feeling part of a community. I liked living in an apartment building in New York City. I liked seeing the different doormen every day, or catching a glimpse of the beautiful family down the hall with children and dogs and the detritus of life spilling out their front door. I liked dashing through the hospital corridors, recognizing so many people that I knew: the respiratory therapists and anesthesiologists and patient transporters and senior attending physicians and everyone in between.

I like it when this egg farmer says, "See you next week." And she and I both know that she will.

Eggs are fragile, eggs break. Eggs are irreplaceable when they do break. Humpty-Dumpty and all that. Yet somehow, in this small transaction between my egg farmer and me, when I connect my food purchases to a person or a place, we strengthen our sense of community. We are not so fragile anymore, so alone.

SIDEBAR: Don't Eggs Raise Cholesterol?

Depending on the day of the week and which newspaper or medical journal I pick up to read, I may learn that, this week, eggs are either a good source of cholesterol or a bad source of cholesterol. The jury is out, and frequently fickle. Simply, the eggs that I use for challah are from chickens and they contain cholesterol. And we, as humans, get our cholesterol from both exogenous sources (outside sources, such as chicken eggs) and from endogenous sources (we make it ourselves). There is good cholesterol and there is bad cholesterol: the good cholesterol helps to lower the bad cholesterol in our bodies. We care about this because high cholesterol can raise our risk of heart disease, and as I've already mentioned, heart disease is the number one killer of women. I care about women's health; ergo, I care about cholesterol. And I eat eggs.

Once again, it's about balance. The recipe only calls for two eggs, and the recipe once baked makes two loaves of challah. Each loaf can be further divided into at least fifteen to twenty pieces of challah. In other words, not so much egg per piece. Not too much to worry about, re: cholesterol. Sometimes, I'll fry up an egg for breakfast, and I frequently use one to make vegetable fried rice. Sometimes I make hard-boiled eggs; I really just like to use that cool metal contraption from my childhood that slices the hard-boiled eggs thinly, much like a mandolin. Eggs are a good, cheap source of protein and, as an added benefit, a great source of choline (great for brain development), lutein (great for preventing eye diseases such as cataracts), and vitamin D (great for bone health—think osteoporosis).

Salt: Buy Morton, the one in the blue canister

I only knew of one kind of salt until I lived in New York City. I knew of Morton iodized table salt in the trusty blue canister. My mother always kept a canister of it tucked up in the cupboard on the second shelf, hidden behind the spices. I think she still does. And I felt right at home early on in my mother-in-law's kitchen when I found the same canister in the corresponding cupboard. Maybe it's the universal sign for moms.

The recipe called for two teaspoons of salt, and these two teaspoons would be Morton iodized salt for my first challah. As I became more comfortable with the recipe and the process, I tried different varieties of each ingredient, including salt. I tried kosher salt, both coarse and fine grain. I tried fine sea salt. But more often than not, I returned to my trusty blue canister, iodized table salt.

Kosher salt might have appeared to be the natural choice, at least the appropriate choice. After all, this is challah, a Jewish bread. Interesting to note that this salt gets its name from its original purpose: to make meats kosher by extracting the blood. Unfortunately, this seemingly obvious choice of salt was too coarse for me to work with in this recipe. It didn't dissolve thoroughly, evenly. I love to use it when I want to play chef, when I am finishing a dish with a dash of salt, when I am making a homemade salad dressing. But for baking, this coarse, cool and of-the-moment salt did not make the cut.

Also, I've learned that not all kosher salts are the same. I have learned that different brands of kosher salt are denser than others, that some are just plain saltier. This requires variations in the amount used, not necessarily just what's stated in the recipe. Alas, that uncertainty unnerves me. I am all for approximating an amount of an ingredient, but I want to do that of my own accord, not because the recipe might have actually been formulated with a different brand/product in mind. That's too stressful for me and runs counter to my desire to keep it simple.

I have also tried sea salt, *fleur de sel.* It had looked so pretty in the little jar on the shelf in my favorite food shop. I had bought some as a gift. Then I thought, *why not? Why not try it myself?* It didn't work. It was too high-end, too fancy, for plain challah. It made my bread taste salty, if that's possible. Sometimes things meant as a gift should retain their specialness.

Once again, I rushed back to that trusty blue canister.

SIDEBAR:
Isn't salt bad for your blood pressure?

My challah recipe calls for two teaspoons of salt. Whenever I hear the word salt, I instinctively stifle the urge to cringe. I have childhood memories of a grandfather on a salt-restricted diet for his heart health and his daughter—my mother—for whom everything was black or white. Salt or no salt? She chose no salt. And since actions speak louder than words, I had absorbed this no-salt attitude almost without realizing it.

My mistake.

Salt is crucial for us, for our bodies, and definitely for making good bread. And I wanted to make good challah. No, I want to make great challah, challah whose aroma enveloped everyone in the vicinity of our kitchen on any given Friday, challah to lose yourself in, challah to find yourself in.

And for that, I need salt. Why? Normally, I understood salt to add flavor, or to enhance existing flavor, but in bread, salt does so much more: salt reins in the yeast. Specifically, salt stops the process of fermentation, or proofing, of the yeast. This slowdown is important because it allows the gluten in the bread to strengthen.

I need salt for challah, but not too much: one cause of heart disease is high blood pressure, also known as hypertension. Many of us will be diagnosed with hypertension by the time we are grandparents. In susceptible individuals, too much salt can increase your blood pressure, so it should be fairly straightforward for these individuals: cut back your salt intake, lower risk for heart disease. That's not so simple these days: most of our diets contain excess amounts of sodium, and salt is the most common way that we consume our sodium. Why? Most of us eat large quantities of processed foods, and many of us eat out at restaurants. Processed foods and restaurants notoriously use an abundance of sodium. Home cooking is not the culprit here; I add salt to my recipe without a moment's hesitation because the sprinkle I add is nothing compared to the quantities in a can of Progresso soup or a box of Kraft Macaroni and Cheese.

Salt isn't all bad. In fact, salt has become a vehicle for delivering iodine into our diets. Iodine is an essential trace mineral—essential because we need it, trace because we don't need that much of it. Simply put: our bodies need iodine, especially our thyroids. What an elegant solution and public health bonanza: fortify salt, and therefore, cheaply improve the lives of billions.

One of our most important organs, the thyroid, produces two hormones that we need to regulate our bodies' metabolism, triiodothyronine (T3) and thyroxine (T4). In order to produce these two fundamental hormones, the thyroid requires iodine. These two hormones essentially control how much energy our bodies can burn: not enough hormone and we don't burn enough energy; too much hormone and we burn too much. And every organ system experiences the effects: too much hormone, and everything speeds up—think faster heart rates, irregular periods, and weight loss; not enough hormone, and everything slows down—think constipation and fatigue, for example.

It was difficult for me to imagine someone's thyroid not working properly until I saw firsthand an abnormal thyroid. A picture is worth a thousand words, or so I've always been told. I remember sitting in an outpatient clinic early on in medical school, just a student in a small cramped exam room, waiting to take the history of the next scheduled patient. When she walked in, I looked up and the first impression I had was of her bulbous neck. My patient had a huge mass dead center in her neck. This is what thyroid disease can look like. Thank goodness for the trusty blue canister that someone thought to fortify with iodine.

Mise En Place: Get Organized; It's Key

When you are ready to begin, you need to get everything out. You need to set up. You need your *mise en place*. Chefs have their *mise en place*—French for "putting in place." Literally, setting up everything ahead of time, putting everything in its place.

I place all six ingredients on the counter before I begin. It makes everything so much easier. I didn't learn this from reading food memoirs, though I've got an entire bookshelf of them. Rather, I learned this as a physician at the bedside, in the hospital when I prepared to insert a large IV—specifically, one known as a central line—into a patient for this first time. Beyond terrified, I stood almost paralyzed. After all, it had been the thought of having to do this very procedure that had kept me up for weeks before starting my internship training. I had almost convinced myself that I would never be able to complete such an invasive and potentially painful procedure.

Fortunately, an exceptional woman stood next to me at the patient's bedside. She was a third-year resident in her last year of training and very calm, cool, and collected. Rather Grace Kelly–like, I thought. A woman just a few years older than I, whom I would come to respect tremendously, a woman who would come to teach me so many of the skills I learned that first year of my medical residency. I watched silently as she set up the *mise en place* right there on the patient's bed, on top of the patient's sheets, just next to the patient: she set about creating a sterile field (area) for us to insert this very large IV into the patient's femoral artery (main artery of the thigh). She began by laying down a plasticized blue sheet. On top of that, she carefully arranged all the supplies that we would need for the procedure: the needles, gauze, and various little vials and tubes. If something would need to be opened later, she opened it now. She made it easy. She made it organized. I felt myself calming down; I felt my confidence returning.

After that experience, I copied her. Every time I needed to insert a central line during my residency, I set up my *mise en place* and successfully inserted the IV. I did this every time I went on to teach the residents and medical students on my team, as well.

Years later, practicing women's health in Cleveland, I learned the value of *mise en place* again. Here, I did Pap smears every day in clinic. I had to do this invasive and potentially uncomfortable procedure on young women (maybe their first time), on old women (perhaps changed by menopause), on morbidly obese women, and on everyone in between. A really cool gynecologist I worked with patiently assisted me one day when I couldn't easily do the Pap smear. I fretted, anxious and frustrated with myself, and feeling badly for the patient—who, incidentally, had a great reservoir of patience. What I remember most: this doctor, in her Eileen Fisher–like clothes, one long braid down her back, clogs on her feet, paused before pulling up a stool to help me, looked me directly in the eye, and told me to get myself situated first, to make sure the examination table was at the height that I needed it to be, that all my tools were easily within reach. I was taking care of me first so that I could quickly and efficiently take care of my patient.

And now, many years later, it's how I approach making challah. Setting up a *mise en place* helps me mitigate my anxiety, my worry. Not something I like to admit: I worry a lot. So I like to get out the six ingredients, the bowl, and the spoon before I begin to make the dough. If it's only me that day, I usually just place everything on the counter. If, however, I will be making challah with other women that day, I usually take a moment to transfer the ingredients: I place the requisite number of eggs in a small glass bowl and pour a little salt in smaller glass bowl. I do the same for the sugar. Everything organized, everything gathered and displayed, everything ready to go.

If I make challah at someone else's home, I like to bring over a big wicker basket filled with all of the ingredients—a little bit like Red Riding Hood, but there you have it. I transfer the sugar and salt to small glass containers with tops and place the eggs in a travel-safe yellow plastic egg crate. The crate holds six eggs; my husband brought it home for me from a farmer in the Central Valley one day. The perfect present.

SIDEBAR: Cool tools make it so much more fun

***The Bowl**. Usually I use a large glass bowl. Sometimes I use a metal bowl, sometimes a white plastic bowl, but I choose glass as my go-to. It seems more environmentally friendly and I like to see the ingredients as they blend together. Once the dough has risen, I like to see the dough fill the bowl.*

When I have friends come over to bake, they often bring their own bowls. It's amusing to see what they choose. Once, a friend who had never made challah brought over a beautiful, scalloped-edged wooden salad bowl. It added a festive air to the occasion.

The Measuring Cups.
Ten years into making challah, I've just learned from a friend that I had the wrong measuring cups for the liquid ingredients. The measuring cups for the dry ingredients—in this case, flour—worked, just not for the liquid ingredients. "You know these are the wrong kind of measuring cups?" she asked gently. The wrong measuring cups, after a decade of making challah? Technically, she was correct. There are dry measuring cups and liquid measuring cups. I didn't know this. The dry ones would be your cute stackable cups—you know, the ¼-cup, ⅓-cup, ½-cup, and 1-cup measuring cups. I have a set of stainless steel measuring cups like this, and I was using them for liquid, too. The correct ones for liquid would be similar to Pyrex measuring cups.

Fortunately, I have a collection of Pyrex measuring cups, all different sizes. A one-cup, a two-cup, even an old four-cup I pilfered long ago from my parents' house. Or maybe my mom gave it to me when I moved into my first post-college apartment. God, I loved that apartment. Four hundred dollars a month, and all mine. I liked that it was several floors up in an old walk-up; somehow I felt safer. I liked that my twin brother rented his own first apartment across the hall. I liked the old French doors in the living room that opened in from the covered porch. The same French doors that burst open during a snowstorm one freezing winter Sunday morning when my man was in town for the weekend.

Regardless, that four-cupper has served me in the kitchen in my first apartment, that tiny one-bedroom in my hometown; it has served me in the kitchen my husband and I so lovingly renovated in Cleveland just prior to moving across the country; it has served me in our sunny kitchen here in Los Angeles. It is part of my story now.

These three measuring cups vary in height and size and, as a result, the amount of bubbles produced by the proofing yeast varies in each. Why, I wondered, did the same amount of yeast yield so many bubbles in this cup but not that cup? Was one cup better than the other? Would yeast formed in one cup make better bread than yeast formed in another, different sized cup? Actually, to be truthful, the first time that I switched to the four-cup-sized cup instead of the two-cup-sized cup, and the bubbles did not overflow up past the top, I assumed that I had done something wrong. Perhaps I had added too much water? Perhaps somehow the water I used was too hot? Perhaps I hadn't used enough yeast? I threw the batch away and started over, but the problem recurred. It took a few times of me throwing away a perfectly good mixture to realize that, ah . . . maybe it was not something that I did. Perhaps there was yet another obvious, external, explanation.

This was a big lesson for me. It took making challah again and again to realize that when something goes wrong, it is not always because I did something wrong. "Sorry" used to be one of my favorite words. A guy friend of mine bet me in high school that I couldn't stop saying sorry. "Sorry," I replied. Alas, reflexively, I still want to blame myself first, to assume that I must have done something wrong.

The explanation for how the yeast rises in the Pyrex cups of different sizes was embarrassingly obvious in hindsight. A lesson in basic physics: mass and volume, different diameters and all that. My two-cup Pyrex measuring cup is taller and narrower than my old four-cup Pyrex measuring cup; the amount of bubbles made in the two-cup are taller, and the amount of bubbles made in the four-cup spread out more in this wider and shorter measuring cup, looking like less, even though they are the same amount. You'd think a person who took so many years of science classes—starting with biology in ninth grade with a teacher and his basset hound, all the way through those myriad of advanced science classes in medical school—would know this. But I didn't. Not really. I threw out a lot of yeast mixtures before I figured it out.

Step Three:

Proofing the Yeast

Mix yeast, sugar, and warm water together in small bowl; let stand approximately ten minutes. This mixture will start to bubble.

What makes bread different than any other flat flour-based product? What gives it its heft and life? Yeast. Yeast allows the bread to rise. Yeast is a living organism. But yeast can't do it on its own. Yeast is a team player: it must be proofed in warm water and a bit of sugar. Yeast is a fungus, and therefore to grow it needs both warm water for moisture and sugar for food. When yeast proofs, it has that customary "yeasty" smell, fresh and doughlike. It bubbles and gurgles. There is no mistaking that something is happening, a science experiment right in my own kitchen. No goggles required.

Since yeast is a living organism, it can't stay active forever. It needs food or it will die. So you might go through all that hard work to make challah, only to have the dough not rise. Ancient bakers figured out that, through the process of fermentation, certain yeast species could convert carbohydrate to carbon dioxide. These carbon dioxide molecules cause the dough to rise, or expand, as the gas creates air pockets. When baked, the yeast dies and these air pockets "set." The resulting challah has a wonderful soft texture. Chewy. Lighter than a cracker. Other foods ferment as well: grapes into wine and cabbage into kimchi, for example.

Technically, you don't have to proof the yeast if it has been preserved in the refrigerator. You could just ago ahead, skip that step, and follow along with the recipe. But I say it's best not to temp fate; I always proof my yeast. I want to be sure that it is viable.

For this proofing step, the recipe states: *mix yeast and sugar in warm water.* I add the warm water to the yeast and sugar mixture, all in a measuring cup. Then I leave the measuring cup sitting on the counter while I prepare for the next step. The mixture within does its thing while I do mine. When I make challah with other women, we frequently line up our mixtures alongside each other's on the counter, a modern sculpture of different Pyrex measuring cups. Sunlight reflects through the glass, casting shadows across the countertop, momentarily interrupting our work.

Despite all my best efforts, sometimes the yeast doesn't proof. Sometimes the water remains a murky claylike color with no bubbles, no effervescence. I used to use the yeast mixture anyway, thinking that in these modern times, my refrigerated yeast would carry the day. But the resulting challah lacked some unspecified lightness. It didn't matter if the rest of the ingredients were superlative, or if my technique was flawless. Less-than-ideal yeast results in less-than-ideal challah.

The Art of Patience:
Let Yeast Mixture Stand Approximately Ten Minutes.

I took every conceivable art class as a child; pottery was my favorite. I just liked all of the natty tools I got to use to work with the wet clay, and I liked painting a glaze on my piece and waiting while it went into the kiln. The shiny finished product was never really what I thought it would be. For my tenth birthday, I requested a subscription to *Architectural Digest*. Later, there was never really a doubt that, despite trying out many different majors, I would study art history in college. My closest friends all had serious, worthy majors, or so I thought, while I found my joy in classes like "Color," playing with little pieces of colored paper, an X-Acto knife and a pot of rubber glue. I felt a little guilty, watching my friends poring over political science tomes. I thought I needed a more respectable major; I worried what my parents thought and how I would support myself after graduation. Even later, I nominate Histology as the best class in my first year of medical school, hands down: we peered into our microscopes (I had borrowed my boyfriend's father's microscope, and I married that boyfriend the next year, guaranteeing myself lifetime access to that wonderful contraption), checking out the beautifully colored slides of different tissues, different pathogens. Different stains produce these different colorations and patterns—very abstract usually, mostly Pollack-like. Rarely neat and clean like a Mondrian. I easily got lost looking at these patterned slides. And later still, once I became a physician, I understood that to successfully practice medicine, I needed to approach it as an art, not just as a science.

Proofing yeast exemplifies practicing an art, not just a science. The recipe says to let it stand for approximately ten minutes. On my first day of making challah, unsure of what the "approximately" was all about, I did just that. I looked up at the clock on the microwave and noted the time. Ten minutes is a very long time to just wait. And wait. The digital numbers switched themselves in slow motion the longer I stared at them. I didn't know what I was looking for that day. I had no idea when exactly the yeast/sugar/water mixture became more than just three individual ingredients, and I felt I had to know. Standing alone in the kitchen, staring at a murky mixture that proffered no answers, I needed outside reassurance. I needed Alexa to help guide me, so somewhere just shy of ten minutes I called her, my friend in New York City who had prompted me to make challah in the first place. It was one of four calls I made to her that day.

She laughed when I called. "Wait," she said. "Just wait."

"How do I know that it's been enough time?" I asked. "What am I waiting for? What's the point of ten minutes?"

She spoke of patience, of simply waiting, of relinquishing control. I could do nothing to control whether the yeast proofed and how long it would take. Except I could wait. I could give it time to work with the sugar and warm water. (*I really hate waiting. For anything.*) The yeast would proof, she said, and there was nothing to do but wait and believe that it would. So I waited and watched the digital numbers on the microwave and watched the murky water bubble and rise up in my Pyrex measuring cup. When ten minutes had elapsed, I declared that the yeast was proofed, but I didn't really know. You never really know.

An art, then, not a science. Not measurable exactly. One thousand challahs and counting. Clearly, I am learning to wait. Since then, I have learned to trust my instincts. I no longer look at the clock. I no longer worry whether the yeast will proof, or when it will proof. I don't rely on external clues. I look inward. I just *know*. Knowledge is power, or so I've been taught. Just knowing when the yeast mixture is ready to add to the dough is powerful. It allows me to own the experience. This time that I take for myself once a week to make challah becomes my time—time I know is mine for the taking.

My Orthodox friends take this one step further: "Beth," they tell me, "patience is really just realizing that G-d decides the speed. G-d decides when the yeast is proofed."

And probably everything else.

Now, in yet another house with yet another adjusted hot water heater, I turn on the tap. I let it briefly heat up while I gather the ingredients and bowl and spoon that I will need. I measure out the yeast and the sugar, believing that the water will be warm enough when I am ready to use it. I usually go by how the mixture looks. At first, the yeast and sugar turn the water into a taupe-like cocktail. While I prepare to measure and mix the other ingredients, the mixture undergoes a metamorphosis. Bubbles begin to appear on the surface, small and perfectly spherical. If the sun is shining that morning, they glitter like small diamonds, casting a kaleidoscope of light across the countertop. The watery mixture gains in clarity as the bubbles gather; the more bubbles, the less murky the water.

The Art of Humility:
Let Yeast Mixture Stand Approximately Ten Minutes.

Waiting for the yeast to proof exercises more than patience. Waiting also exercises humility. It's the greatest of all character traits, according to the Talmud. Humility supplants the ego, pushes away the tendency for self-centeredness. With humility comes the ability to have empathy. Proofing the yeast, perhaps the greatest step in making challah, is not about me, about how well I make the challah, or how well I do anything else, for that matter. Proofing the yeast is out of my control: the mixture *will* start to bubble (or perhaps not) once these three ingredients are mixed together. And that's a good thing.

During my medical training, many opportunities reminded me about what is and what is not out of my control. On our on-call days (and nights), we admitted patients all throughout the day and into the night, until we were "capped" at our admission quota of five patients per on-call team. Late one night in my fourth year of medical school, at about 3 a.m., I worked on a write-up of a woman who had come in earlier in the day. She was in bad shape, and I was indescribably exhausted. My primary goal became singular: an impressive write-up to present in a few hours. Rounds would begin first thing in the morning and I wanted to impress my attending physician; I didn't want to be singled out for having prepared an incomplete write-up. I wanted to be top of the class. Perhaps, I mused as I tried to piece together the details of her history and physical, labs and radiographic imaging, the patient assigned to me had Virchow's triad, a blood clot in the setting of a hypercoagulable (more likely to clot) state, secondary to likely cancer. ("Did you see all of those dark spots on her CT scan?" the tactless radiology resident on call had noted earlier that night. "Her abdomen lights up like a goddamned Christmas tree.") Perhaps she didn't have cancer after all; perhaps she had an infection, maybe Fitz-Hugh-Curtis Syndrome, a rare complication of pelvic inflammatory disease secondary to a sexually transmitted disease. I had the audacity to presume that if I could just determine the problem, it could be fixed. Controlled.

That woman is dead now. She died a few months after that hospital admission, from complications due to metastatic pancreatic cancer. I think of her sometimes as I stand in the light of the kitchen window on Friday mornings, watching the yeast bubble uncontrollably. She was the age that I am now as I type this. I can't imagine receiving a similar diagnosis now. Oh, I know, we all are only going to live for so long, and I know that we should cherish each and every day. But I don't. I forget. I sweat the small stuff. I can't imagine being told that I have a few months to live, that I won't see my children start high school or learn to drive or fall in love for the first time. And yet we gave her that diagnosis. We told her that she only had a few months to live. Her grace and dignity in the face of an incurable, relentless, and painful disease humbled me then, and continues to humble me now. We couldn't cure her, but we could work with her to make her comfortable, help her through her final journey. We could learn from her example. Dying, too, is an art, and not merely a science.

BAKING

Step One:

The First Big Mix

Meanwhile, in a large mixing bowl, mix together eggs, salt, sugar, oil and two cups flour.

I use six ingredients. No more. No less. I don't make chocolate chip challah. I don't make cinnamon challah. I don't make challah dyed various colors or any of the other millions of interesting flavored and/or colored challahs out there. I make just pure, unadulterated, plain challah. Whether I celebrate a banner day or mourn a lousy day, I don't vary the ingredients.

I want it to remain simple and predictable. I don't want to confuse this experience, this moment, with superfluous ingredients and flavors. I am not wondering whether I should add food coloring to enhance the look of the bread. Instead, I am reveling in a few minutes of *not thinking*. No longer needing to look at the recipe, I just work on autopilot. I can savor the act of making challah now without worrying about the process itself. It is like there is an invisible sous chef working alongside with me, making the six ingredients appear on the kitchen counter. The yeast begins proofing before I even realize it. The mixing bowl is ready and waiting for me. While the yeast proofs, I start in with the first big mix. In a large bowl, I add in the eggs, salt, sugar, oil, and half of the flour (about two cups' worth).

For years, I just placed the ingredients in the bowl without too much forethought. If the sugar canister sat closest at hand, sugar went in first. If I could easily reach the egg carton, I cracked the eggs in first. (They're best at room temperature, by the way; I try to remember that and usually I don't.) I thought that the order I added these ingredients didn't matter. It was all going to be mixed together, anyway, so I put each ingredient in as I grabbed it, and once they were all in the bowl, I began to stir them all together. I didn't connect the end product to the process until a bright and sunny Friday morning when I watched my friend Sarah make challah by my side.

Sarah and I met one afternoon while leaning against a red brick wall of our local public school waiting to pick up our children. She is bright and inquisitive, and much more thoughtful in how she made her challah dough. It wasn't so much the order in which she added the ingredients that gave me pause; rather, it was what she was doing while she added the ingredients: stirring, constantly stirring. In went the sugar, then the eggs. Stir, break up the yolks, and blend in the sugar. Don't stop stirring. In went the salt, more stirring, then the oil, finally the flour. And all the while, she never stopped stirring.

The consistency of her dough at this point differed from the consistency of my dough. Her dough looked smoother, less lumpy than mine. I liked hers better. And it turned out several hours later that her bread looked better than mine, too. It looked more "professional," less clumsy in appearance. Shamelessly, I copied her behavior. I began to stir the ingredients as I added them instead of waiting until I had placed all five ingredients in the bowl. I began to start with the oil and eggs, making it easier for me to mix in the sugar and salt. For consistency, of course—a better texture, a smoother texture, a more elegant dough. I've since learned that it's not the order in which I add the ingredients, it's that I keep *stirring* as I add them.

So now I always stir the ingredients as I pour them in, though I am not always meticulous about the order in which I add them to the bowl. It always works out, whether I start with the sugar or the oil or the flour or the eggs, or whether I add two heaping cups of flour or exactly two cups. Just get in the game. It's not all or nothing.

I don't care if you run for thirty minutes a day or break it up into ten minutes increments here or there. I do care, though, that you are active for thirty minutes a day, and not just because the Department of Health and Human Services issued guidelines in 2008 with these widely adopted recommendations for 150 minutes of moderate exercise weekly. It's simpler than that. It's just a matter of *you* . . . getting in the game.

SIDEBAR: The Perfect Spoon

The Spoon. *I originally chose to use a great big wooden spoon, replete with a large carved animal at the top of the handle, a gift from my brother.*

He bought it in Africa years ago, while in the Peace Corps.

I got a kick out of making the same bread that has been made every Friday for nearly four thousand years, originally on a distant continent, an ocean and world away, with a spoon that is also from a faraway place. Alas, my challah making has outlived that particular spoon's life. For a while, then, I tried every other spoon I had in my kitchen drawer—long-handled ones and wooden ones and Teflon ones, narrow-handled ones and short ones and squat ones. It had to feel right in my hand, in the bowl, and in the dough.

Stirring dough takes strength and takes a consistent hand. I needed the right spoon to help with that task, and I couldn't find it for a while. I struck out at the gourmet grocery store, at Bed Bath & Beyond, at Williams-Sonoma. Did I mention that I wanted three of them? I wanted to be able to share the perfect spoon—that's half the fun: when another woman comes over to make challah, I want her to have the right spoon, too.

I kept looking. And one day, there it was—my spoon—at yet another grocery store, this one gourmet and off my usual path, in an aisle I don't usually frequent. It was a bright yellow spoon, perfectly smooth silicone. Exactly what I had looked for—not too long or too thin or too anything. And the store had three. Surely that was a sign: I bought them immediately. With the right spoon in hand, I can just focus on the task of making challah.

BAKING

Step Two:

The First Blessing

Now would be a great time to say to yourself, "I am making this dough in the merit of _____" (name someone . . . maybe a friend who is sick that week, or someone you are happy for, sad for, mad at, etc.).

The Big Mix offers a special moment at the start of the challah making process: the chance to bless someone. I learned about this idea on a trip to Israel, where I had the opportunity to make challah with a group of women. I went to Israel for the first time when I was 42. Rather appropriate, since the number 42 is the answer to the "ultimate question of life, the universe and everything" (from Douglas Adams's *The Hitchhiker's Guide to the Galaxy*, a favorite in our house). Jackie Robinson wore the now-retired baseball number 42. My children's first school bus was #42. I believe in signs; I believe that they are all around us. That summer, the number 42 was a sign.

On a hot Sunday morning in late July, I left my husband and children alone for nine days, for the first time since the birth of my first child twelve years earlier. Part of a journey of women chosen to embark on an immersion experience with other women from around North America, we were a pack of forty. We departed from Terminal 3 at LAX, representing a wide spectrum of Jewish women from Southern California, from Reform to Orthodox Judaism and everything in between. Fifteen hours nonstop on El Al—fifteen uninterrupted hours all to myself, previously unimaginable. I read two books, watched a movie and woke up over the Black Sea. Looking out over Eastern Europe in the early morning hours while most of the plane's inhabitants still slumbered made me uncomfortable. I had long heard so many stories from my own grandparents, and friends' grandparents, about the oppression that Jews faced in Eastern Europe. My husband's grandmother's family smuggled her out of Russia in a hay cart. She was only three, her mouth gagged to prevent her from crying and possible detection. I felt safer once we reached Israeli airspace: I figured the odds of my safety actually would increase in a country with sophisticated technology and a deep desire to defend themselves, soldiers armed and ready.

And then we landed.

I had been told many people would kiss the ground when we landed; they did. And before we landed, they chanted morning prayers, gathering at the back of the plane, in the galley, and spilling into the aisles. The energy at the airport alone was enough to let me know that I was in a different place, a different space. Ben Gurion Airport, the gateway to our homeland and that of so many other peoples, is like no other. It's loud and crowded, filled with Jews and Christians and Muslims (and probably other religions too)—all coming to this tiny land no bigger than New Jersey, all coming *home*. I spent that one week in Israel primarily in the Old City of Jerusalem. Before we drove into that city on a hill, its lights twinkling in the dark sky, we saw the Galilee and rafted down the Jordan River—so close to Syria and Jordan, just on the other side of those tall mountains. What had loomed so large in my mind instead reminded me of the movie, *Honey I Shrunk the Kids*. I couldn't stop staring at those mountains— all those Middle Eastern countries, all that hatred, and I could see it all with my own eyes. Practically touch them.

When we got to the Old City, I walked on the narrow streets, perhaps the very streets my ancestors walked, in and around the Western Wall, the Kotel, perhaps at the very site that they might have prayed. I made challah with a rebbetzin who most definitely still makes challah the way my ancestors might have made it. She taught me to make challah in the merit of someone. We ate dinner one evening on a rooftop overlooking the Western Wall, directly facing the Temple Mount. It was the same night as Ramadan. As we said our prayers in Hebrew and prepared to break bread together, the lights went on in and around the Temple Mount, signaling the end of that day's fast and the time to eat for those observing Ramadan. We could hear their calls to prayer as we too prayed. A different language, a different prayer. Perhaps for the same purpose.

Each week since that trip, I say to myself that I will make this week's challah in the merit of someone, maybe a friend who's sick or someone I am upset with or thrilled for, or just because. For my brother-in-law, whose cherished colleague finally passed away after a long and protracted illness. For my best friend's husband, just out of surgery, again. For my child studying hard at school that week. When it's just me making bread, alone, I have recently started to say this dedication aloud, to own it, to make it real. Perhaps if it's truly "out there" in the universe, it will matter.

I knead for my needs.

I hit a wall last week, driving my minivan. It was pouring rain, slippery, and I slammed into a wall and smashed the front end of my car. I have no idea what happened (they think I slid on oil on the wet pavement, but who knows), and I sat there trembling for five minutes unable to do anything, call anybody. But it was a Friday morning. A challah-making morning. For the first time in ten years, I made challah in the merit of myself. And, shockingly, I felt better. Yes, I always make it in the merit of someone, now that I know that I should. But sometimes I do things just because I should. Even if I don't believe in it. And I never really knew if it mattered that I made the dough in the merit of someone. But that Friday afternoon, when the minivan had been towed, the challah had been made, and my kids and their friends were excited to eat it, I felt good. I felt better. I felt *okay.*

I will try not to forget to say that I am making challah in the merit of someone again. It matters. Now I know.

When I make challah with other women, this moment has the capacity to bind us together. Much like the dough itself coming together, this story each one of us shares aloud now brings us together. This moment elevates the whole process, and it takes but a moment.

Recently, I made the dough on a Friday morning before one of my children took an important math test, one that required more effort than usual. Thinking of him and all of the hard work that he had put forth, I paused with the measuring spoon of salt high above the bowl, and I stated aloud that I was making the dough this week in his honor. I felt a little foolish, alone in my kitchen, speaking out loud to no one physically present. More importantly, I felt inspired and even a little bit empowered. He had worked hard for this test; I wanted to honor that. So I did. Of course, I secretly hoped that a lone neighbor walking by or perhaps the gardener working outside did not catch me with a spoon raised in the air, lips moving.

Step Three:

Fertilization

Add yeast mixture (1) to flour mixture (2).

To life, to life, *L'chaim!* I always feel a moment of joy as I prepare to pour the bubbly yeast mixture into the emerging dough. Together, the yeast and sugar and warm water have become something new, something different, something alive. Sometimes I think I should wave a wand—and chant abracadabra. Magic, or alchemy, name it what you will, this moment is holy. Quite simply, first I had dry, loose yeast, sugar, and water. Now, I have a living, bubbling concoction that will spark the dough, allowing what could have been flat to now rise up. With the yeast, I get a three-dimensional loaf of bread. Like Magellan setting off to circumnavigate the earth: instead of falling off a flat disc into nothingness, he sails on.

Wonderment

The wonderment of watching something come alive: this is not the moment to check a text, answer a call, indulge in a random thought. This is a moment to be present, to be aware, to indulge in some awe. Until I started making challah, I didn't have too many moments of awe on a regular basis. One startling moment, though, occurred the first time I watched *someone* come alive. Flash back to third year of medical school, while I participated in a two-month rotation in obstetrics and gynecology. During that rotation, I attended many births, privileged to participate in some. Each experience was special, each unique. The first one, though, will be forever etched in my mind: the mom, the baby, the lights in the room, two doors down on the right from the nurses' station, all those beeping machines. It dawned on me, as I walked into that room, that I had never seen a birth. Well, an actual birth, in real life, as opposed to the movies or TV. I didn't grow up on or near a farm and get to see any births. I didn't even have a pet that had birthed a pup or a kitten. No, this would be my first witnessed birth.

I went into the room. I stood to the side. She had been in labor for a while; it was well into night now. My celadon-green scrubs were beginning to feel like a second skin, sticking to me, my feet aching in my black Dansko clogs. I was keyed up, anxious and very much present. Here was a pregnant woman. Here was her man. And if all went well, here a baby would soon make three. My eyes remained glued to the various monitors, as though that incessant beeping might tell me something. And still she labored. Shifts changed, new nurses began their ministrations. And still she labored. All the while, she tolerated my presence, my questions, my awe. It's indescribable, watching a birth in person for the first time. It just is. It's not like the textbooks or the TV shows: it takes a long time, it's messy. Sometimes it's stressful and sometimes it's boring. All that waiting around—until that moment when, suddenly, words fail.

Have you seen a baby crowning, its little head emerging? I hadn't. Thin wisps of brown hair plastered to her tiny head. A breath taken. Everything else ceased in that brief moment in time between the doctor delivering the baby and the baby taking its first breath. Not a sound, not a thought, not a distraction. We were all *there*. Present and waiting. And then she breathed. This tiny baby breathed. A new life. The nurse shouted out the time of birth. The quiet shattered.

I witnessed many deliveries that month; I caught ten babies (that would be medical parlance for *delivering* ten babies). Each one unique, each birth forever changing those involved. Some were straightforward, textbook really. Some weren't: once, a baby had its umbilical cord wrapped around its neck; once, a baby was born stillborn. Then, I cried. Strange as it might seem, picking up the Pyrex measuring cup and seeing with my own eyes the yeast/sugar/water mixture come alive is a little like being back in that delivery room. A witness to a *living* moment.

It will be messy at first, adding the yeast/sugar/water mixture to the first big mix before adding in the rest of the flour. It may look lumpy and discolored; it may even feel like you're wading through a muddy bog. But life is messy. Sometimes we muddle through, doing the best we can, just hoping to get through another day. Like all those early mornings I sent the kids out to the bus stop in freezing weather, the three of them wearing the requisite gloves and hats and snow pants and boots. But I was always forgetting the scarf. Other mothers always seemed to have their children attired just so on those cold winter mornings—like perfect little packages tied with a bow, their scarves securely fastened, keeping their little necks warm. I could never get it exactly right. But my kids made the bus and got to school; they survived those years just fine. I like to think that the lack of scarf on those cold days has not harmed them.

The same is true here. It's only the first mix. Making challah is a process with many steps. Fortunately, there will be plenty of time to clean up the mess.

BAKING

Step Four:

The Second Big Mix

Add approximately 1½ cups of flour to the mixture. Dough should start to form a ball, separating from the bowl.

The second big mix is just this: add the remaining flour. The six ingredients come together now in a bowl. That's it. Nothing fancy, nothing esoteric, no complicated Cordon Bleu moment.

Except that you must now make a judgment about the flour. Maybe the dough needed 3½ cups last week in order to feel right, but this week maybe it's closer to four cups. Be flexible, go with it. It's a good thing to practice.

For a Type A personality, being flexible is not in my job description. It is one thing for me to tell *you* to take it in stride, to go with the flow, that life is a little imprecise. But for me, no . . . not so much. I want it clearly articulated; I want to know exactly what to expect. I don't want to be surprised. Making challah has become an act of imprecision for me. It has become a weekly reminder that I still need to work on embracing flexibility.

Sometimes the dough requires 3¾ cups of flour, sometimes four. I don't always know. And sometimes I eat one slice of challah, and sometimes I mindlessly finish off whatever's left on the serving platter after dinner. I am not even aware of my actions until the plate is empty, until I feel overly full. And that's frustrating. Why can't I just eat one slice and be done with it?

Why? Because life is messy.

That initial recipe from the JCC in New York City, the one that Alexa had shared with me so long ago, called for *four* cups of flour. Four exactly. Divided into two portions—the first two cups added with the initial ingredients before adding the proofed yeast, and the second two cups added after the proofed yeast. There is no complicated quadratic equation to solve here. Just simply add two cups before and two cups after the yeast.

Professional bakers have a proper way to measure a cup of flour. Professional bakers recognize the precision that is required. I am not a professional baker. I used to think that dipping my one-cup measuring cup in the bag of flour sufficed. Sometimes, I took a knife or spatula and leveled the top just because it seemed more exact and made me feel legitimate, like a real chef. Most times, I didn't. I just dipped. If I had dared to be so imprecise in my chemistry labs in college, certainly there would have been a few more explosions. Fortunately, what serious chefs do is *weigh* their flour—with a scale, no less. Two cups of flour would be a bit more than eight ounces of flour by weight. So last year I bought a really cute little digital scale, thinking I would get serious, too. I haven't touched it yet. Every time I open that particular cupboard and see it sitting there, I feel pangs of guilt. Luckily, my challah recipe, it turns out, does not demand precision.

I didn't grow up baking, my mother didn't bake very often, and I can't remember my grandmothers ever baking. When I started making challah, I didn't necessarily appreciate all that went into baking, the need for precision and for exact amounts of different solids and liquids. My history included watching the older women in my family volunteer in the community, knowing that they spent time in art museums and that they ensured the daily family dinner occurred. But fresh cookies in the cookie jar? Not so often in our house, except for lace cookies (I don't even know their real name; maybe that's it), especially around the winter holidays. Remember Soft Batch cookies, those chocolate chip cookies in the red package? Those were the frequent cookies in our cookie jar. Thus, I didn't know what it meant to actually bake or how to really be a baker. I didn't know what a home smells like when something is baking (though years later I came home to freshly baked lemon squares and brownies).

Making dough now reminds me of being in the lab: measure out a few milliliters of this and mix with a few milliliters of that and watch what happens. I did not always know what reaction to expect in the beaker on the Bunsen burner in lab class after all, and I don't always know now what to expect with the dough. Sometimes the dough feels heavy, sometimes light and fluffy. I don't always know why. The mystery is part of the magic. I've just swapped an apron for those uncomfortable plastic safety goggles, the ones that were always too large and slid down my nose. But the process remains the same.

Back to the big mix: in the beginning, I followed the recipe.

I added two cups of flour before the yeast, followed by two cups after the yeast. It didn't work out so well for me. The dough felt too heavy after I unceremoniously dumped in the second two cups of flour. It actually felt like a heavy lump of clay. I found it difficult to stir the initial dough, difficult to mix in the yeast, difficult to knead. But I didn't question *why* at first. I just assumed that that was how it was supposed to be. And I assumed that the resulting bread—a little heavy, a little dense—was how it was supposed to be. But we know where assumptions lead us. Nowhere.

Perhaps There Is Such a Thing as Too Much of a Good Thing?

It took me a while initially to hone that it is the amount of flour that contributes to heavy dough and subsequent heavy bread. Perhaps, I mused, the fault lay with the water. In those early challah-making years, I used the municipal tap water in Cleveland; maybe that caused the problem. Were there too many minerals? Or maybe not enough? Perhaps the gray weather was to blame. The lake effect in Cleveland exacerbated my headaches; the atmospheric pressure wreaked havoc on my moods, and those of my patients. Perhaps my challah had seasonal affective disorder, too?

I just wanted light and fluffy challah. Was that too much to ask? Yes, it turns out, at first it was too much to ask.

I was asking the wrong questions, looking for the wrong answers—just like one of my patients, a lovely older woman with perfectly coifed gray hair. She came to her initial appointment with me complaining of stomach pain. She sat primly next to my desk, laden with a large brown paper grocery bag overflowing with prescriptions, supplements, and a plethora of vitamins. Furthermore, she told me, she did *everything* for her health. Didn't I see, didn't I understand? Here was the proof, this huge bag, already starting to rip along the seams, bursting with more than thirty bottles.

My patient thought that if a little calcium was good, then surely more was better. She thought that if a little vitamin C was good, then surely more was better. These assumptions of hers actually contributed to her symptoms; she was actually making herself sick. I spent a lot of time with her that first day and over the course of many follow-up visits. We discussed whole foods versus individual nutrients. We discussed the correct dosages of both her requisite prescription and over-the-counter medications. We discussed the benefits of calcium and vitamin C, but not taken in isolation. The benefit comes from whole foods, from their nutrients working together, not in isolation. It's the oatmeal with the blueberries and skim milk, not just taking extra calcium. She got it. She cut back on her excess vitamins, and most of her gastrointestinal symptoms abated.

It turned out that neither the water nor the weather was ruining my bread; I was asking the wrong questions and looking for the wrong answers. Maybe it was something else— the flour, for example, or at the very least, how I was adding it in.

I dared to start the second big mix with adding only 1½ cups of flour instead of the remaining two, and the challah was lighter. Better. Suddenly free, I could add exactly however much flour was needed on that day for that particular dough. So I now always start with 1½ cups for the second big mix; and this is what I advise my fellow challah bakers to do as well. Moreover, I have found that once I put the dough on the countertop to knead, it all works out. If the dough feels too sticky to knead, I add a bit more flour. If it feels just right, I stop: no more flour. Since I can't take out the extra flour, I prefer to start with less initially and then add a little bit as needed. In this way, by following my instincts about the flour, the dough will end up lighter and fluffier. I usually get it right this way, but not always. Once in a while, it still doesn't feel quite right. Now that I have a system, though, for how to correct what bothered me, I don't notice the dough feeling leaden as much. I learned in medical school that there is actually a name for this condition: *anticipatory anxiety*. Seems I suffer from it. I often worry about things that haven't happened yet, that may not actually happen at all. Leaden dough is one of them, and now, fortunately, I can remove that one from the list.

Once you've added the 1½ cups of flour, continue to work the dough in the bowl until it begins to form a ball and separates from the walls of the bowl. The dough will be uneven, maybe even still a bit unblended. Perhaps it will feel a bit sticky. Just wait: all will be taken care of shortly, when you knead the dough.

Such flexibility does not usually work when baking a chocolate cake or peanut butter cookies, or most any baked treat. In general with baking, you have to follow a recipe rather strictly to achieve the desired result. It's the point of writing a recipe down in the first place—and then following it. And yet I find it particularly noteworthy that this challah recipe continues to afford me the opportunity to bend the rules a bit, to modify when modifying is what's called for. Sometimes, that's just life. Sometimes, that's just what this doctor ordered.

Sidebar: A Word About Honey

Sometimes simplicity is just inherent, the right choice, the only choice. However, sometimes I'm tempted to sweeten the deal. Then, I think: honey. I like things sweet and honey does the trick. Want to get something done at work? Want your kids to do something for you? Want something from your partner? I love the adage: "You catch more flies with honey than with vinegar." And, no surprise, challah is the same. Sometimes it's just better when it's sweeter. I learned this firsthand from my friend Marne, the one who had no canola oil. She harvests her own honey. None of those little plastic bears of honey for her. She has the real deal, harvested from a beehive in her backyard.

When she and her husband built their current home years ago, an old beehive fell to the ground. As the story goes, she was told repeatedly to dispose of it, that it was a lost cause, that bees couldn't make honey once their hive had fallen. But Marne refused to believe this. At the time, the media was full of stories about the loss of bees and beehives across the nation, and how this was affecting crops, honey production, and our environment in general.

Marne wasn't going to let the hive die. Not on her watch. After much research, she found a beekeeper to help her save her hive. Each year, the honey changes somewhat, influenced by the flowers blooming in her backyard that year. My family and I have been the beneficiaries.

Most of us need a bit of sweetness to flourish; not all of us are as fortunate as Marne to have it literally at our fingertips. This is one more reason why I believe that making challah is a community act: when women make challah together, we come together over shared stories—and if I'm lucky, even a little fresh homegrown honey.

If and when I add honey, it is here, at the second big mix. It is traditional to add honey at Rosh Hashanah, the Jewish New Year, in order to ensure a year's worth of sweetness. But adding honey to the dough comes at a price. It invariably changes the consistency of my dough at this step. I have had to alter the recipe —usually by adding a bit more flour—to adjust for the increased viscosity, the increased stickiness. Just like in life, when things get sticky, you've got to adapt. Honey reminds me to alter my ways to adjust to this new normal.

BAKING

Step Five:

Kneading the Dough

*Place the dough on a floured surface and knead, lifting up
with one hand and then the other. This should take at least
five minutes as dough becomes increasingly elastic. If necessary, add a bit more flour to the dough if still sticky.
Knead dough into a ball.*

Have you played with Play-Doh recently? So soft, so malle-
able, it's practically irresistible. Kneading challah dough could
give playing with Play-Doh a run for its money. So the dough
is not neon pink or another fabulous color of the rainbow.
And alas, I don't whip out the little rolling pins and cookie
cutters from my kids' old box of Play-Doh paraphernalia. No
crinkly edged scissors to cut with here. Just a large bowlful of
dough, sandy-hued, or maybe looking more like a bowl of
instant oatmeal.

How do you know the dough is ready to knead? How do
you know anything? Sometimes it's just a feeling, an innate
sense that this is the moment. Not armed with years of experience making from-scratch cookies, or working with dough

in any capacity, I relied on Alexa that first time to tell me that I would know that the dough was ready when it separated from the bowl. When suddenly, as if powered by some other life source, it miraculously transformed from a sticky mess into a round ball of dough, fully separating from the walls of the bowl and standing on its own, ready. Driven by an inner power.

The length of time one kneads the dough is difficult to quantify. The original recipe that I used stated that I should knead the dough for up to ten minutes, but to my untrained fingers—and my impatient mind—this seemed too long. After just a few minutes, I had what I thought was a nice ball of dough, so I stopped kneading. Since the finished challah worked out so well, I conveniently forgot that I hadn't actually kneaded it as long as recommended; and I didn't appreciate then that that omission might affect the finished product.

While researching kneading for this book, I realized that I should have kneaded the dough longer, that I should have striven for a different texture, more elastic, smoother, more consistent. So I tried it recently. I just kept kneading. The rhythmic thumps on the kitchen counter felt cathartic. The texture of the dough changed; it matured, it coalesced into something that felt better, correct—how I always imagined dough to feel. Funny, I never really knew what I had been missing until that afternoon. Then I knew with a stunning clarity: I had erred for years in not kneading the dough long enough. Later that evening, my children and their friends exclaimed over the challah. Definitely better, they graded. And alas, I was left just with crumbs to enjoy in the kitchen after dinner, denied my usual leftover challah to nosh on after everyone else went up to bed.

Kneading dough is one of the few times where I can lose myself in the moment. I don't have such a good track record at being present. But it turns out I can be present when pushing down on the ball of dough, pushing the dough away from me with the heel of my hand, then back toward me. Gathering up the stretched dough, pressing it into a ball. And doing it all over again, and then again, and again. Don't overdo it, though; don't pummel it. It's a dance to be done together, not a war to be fought. The dough will tell you when it's ready; you just have to be there and feel the moment. I don't think it's possible to knead the dough too long—probably because I don't have that much patience to just keep going. When all else fails, I knead until my forearm muscles ache.

Sometimes the dough just feels leaden, heavy, no matter how much I knead it. I haven't created the much-needed elasticity, dough with enough air pockets for the carbon dioxide to do its job. Interestingly, my dough consistently feels better to the touch now that I live in LA. It's lighter; it's springier. Is it the sun, is it the water, is it my energy? I don't really question it, other than that I firmly believe that homemade food reflects the person who made it. A happy person makes happy food. Food that just tastes good. And I am happy here.

I like to watch my friends knead dough when we bake challah together. It's so individual. Everyone has a different approach, a different method. Some of my friends are very methodical, turning the dough a perfect ninety degrees every few minutes. Some of my friends tend to the sloppy, just picking up the dough whichever way and haphazardly folding it over somewhat, punching it down, and repeating the process. Watching how they knead the dough tells me so much about who they are: fastidious, sloppy, or somewhere in between. And infinitely predictable: without a doubt, I always know how someone will knead the dough, even if I have never made challah with her before.

So don't think too much and knead on.

BAKING

Step Six:

Rising Up

Place the dough back into oiled bowl, cover and place the covered bowl somewhere warm for 1–1½ hours to rise, approximately doubling in volume.

It took a really cute cowboy up at a ranch on the southern border of Colorado a few years ago to teach me the importance of where and how bread rises. Just putting the dough in a bowl and ignoring it for an hour or two is not sufficient. Where I put the dough to rise matters; how long the dough rises matters.

I had awakened that morning early, as usual. Not wanting to disturb the rest of my crew, I bundled up, grabbed one of the books that I had brought with me and headed up to the main cabin. The couch in front of that oh-so-large-I-could-move-into-it fireplace and a big, steaming cup of coffee had my name on them—or better yet, perhaps I'd abscond with a mug of hot cocoa. Maybe with a marshmallow or two, just because. The most decadent part of any day to me is that hour or so in the early dawn, before anyone else is awake. It's all mine; the world just there waiting for me to enjoy it. The mountain air was so cool that I could easily see my breath, even on that July morning. Across the lawn, several rabbits foraged for their breakfast; birds were just beginning to congregate, the sun sliced through a few tree branches. I gingerly opened the main cabin door.

He knelt by the large hearth, a fire already lit. My footsteps startled him, and he abruptly sat back on his heels. There, spread out before him, were several large industrial-looking bowls filled with the most beautiful dough I had ever seen. I stared. No, I did not stare at him (though he was rather cute, in that mountain-man kind of way, all flannel shirt and cowboy boots). The bowls of dough held me captive.

He laughed at my expression. "What, haven't you seen bread rise?"

Uh, no. I was used to placing my challah dough (the *only* bread that I had ever attempted to bake) back in the bowl that I had made it in, covering it with plastic wrap and leaving it be for an hour to an hour and a half. I vaguely remember hearing something once about keeping the dough warm, so after tightly sealing it and putting a dish towel over it, I used to stick it in the unused microwave oven. This, I figured, would keep it out of sight, safe from whatever else was going to happen in the kitchen for the next hour and a half. And, for at least the hot and humid summer months in the Midwest, when the air conditioning ran continually, putting the dough away like this kept it out of the cool kitchen environment.

My cowboy, as I had come to think of him, quickly disabused me of any of my preconceived ideas about rising dough. Dough, he patiently explained, needs a warm environment in which to rise. And what better place than nestled in the hearth of a fireplace first thing in the morning? Sure enough, when I peeked later that morning, the bowls in front of that fireplace were practically overflowing with the warm, fragrant dough.

The bread we ate that evening around the long communal tables tasted heavenly. It could have been the meal itself. Turns out that this step really affects the end result.

Inspired, I copied that cowboy. First I just tried placing the bowl on the counter above the dishwasher, and conveniently found an excuse to always run the dishwasher Friday mornings. Not such a difficult proposition: as a family of five, we were long on dirty dishes. When the dishwasher clicks on "drying" mode, the countertop always warms up, too. My mother liked to sit up on the warm kitchen counter late into the night, reading a book, sitting pretty above the old steam radiator in our kitchen. Of course, this being Los Angeles, I soon got creative: I opened the back door. Placing the covered bowl on a table on the patio in the sun, I found an even more successful recipe for getting the dough to rise *a lot*. Now, whenever it's especially warm out, I put the dough outside. It's just so much fluffier, and so much more enjoyable to punch down afterward. If it's not warm enough, then I welcome other solutions. A friend of mine has a warming shelf above her stove, a fantastic place to let the challah dough rise. Regardless, practice makes perfect and I am forever searching for great places to let the dough rise.

Practice

What do *we* need to do to rise up to be our best? How do we do this? It's not as though we come with an instruction manual. Even my challah recipe does not specify *how far* the dough should rise. It takes practice, practice, practice. It takes an abundance of trial and error.

Like all women, I have gone through this cycle many times in other realms. Like learning how to write legibly in cursive, like learning how to row so I could be on the crew team, like learning how to suture (to sew up an open incision). This time, too, I would have to rise up in a different direction.

How long the dough rises, not just where it rises, matters. The original recipe I started with ten years ago gave me the option to let it rise *twice*. I could have taken the dough out of the bowl, placed it on a floured countertop and punched it down. Then, I could have put it back in the bowl and let it rise again. My friend Laura practiced this double-rise exercise for many years, although she only made challah intermittently. With four children and many things to do on Fridays, spending all day making bread was neither practical nor convenient. Two rises compromised her ability to make challah; the entire process was just too time-consuming. When we met, I shared my one-rise version. She has since modified her recipe, and now makes challah weekly. Respecting the limitations of time, adapting the recipe to suit her needs, she now continues to make bread.

Spending time with other women, baking challah, has meant that my own challah-making sometimes gets interrupted. Almost by happenstance, I have discovered an intermediate rise, a compromise between two full rises. After the first rise, I still continue on with the recipe as I've always done. But I've learned that if I don't put the prepared braids in the oven right away, and let them just sit on the baking sheet on top of the counter for a little while, the dough expands and the baked challahs are just that much larger, just that much fluffier and more impressive. Either way, with or without a second or partial-second rise, it works.

BAKING

Step Seven:

The Prayers

Preheat oven to 375°. Remove the cover from bowl, place dough on floured surface. Take a small piece of dough (approximately the size of an egg), double wrap in plastic wrap and say the prayer over separating the challah. Discard this piece of wrapped dough and continue on.

As with many mitzvot, there is a blessing to recite along with the act of separating the challah. Historically, challah is not the braided bread, the end product, but rather the piece that we *separate* from the dough when making the bread. *Hafrish challah* is the Hebrew term for separating the challah—all this fuss just for a little piece of dough about the size of an egg.

Now, another moment of transformation, though this time, more for me than for the bread itself. I break off a little piece and recite a prayer after the dough has risen and before I braid it. I always feel my blood pressure lower when I pause to say this prayer—I feel physically better, calmer, for reciting these words:

Baruch Ata A-Do-Nay Elo-haynu Melech Ha-Olam Asher Kidishanu B'Mitzvotav V'Tziyvanu L'Hafrish Challah.
(Hebrew transliteration)

Blessed are You, Lord, our G-d, Ruler of the Universe, Who has sanctified us with Your commandments and commanded us to separate the Challah.

I understand transformation. The first time I wrote my name in a chart as *Doctor* Ricanati is etched deeply in my mind. In that moment, I underwent my own transformation. The nurses' station on the second-floor General Medicine ward that day was overly warm, bathed in the morning sunlight bursting through the tall windows on that old, long floor. I was overwhelmed by the din and activity, by the sheer number of people crowded around the nurses' station after morning rounds. Everybody seemed to know what he or she was doing, why they were there, what their purpose was. Except me. *What was I doing there?* I wanted to meld into the shadows, hide behind the floor clerk, slip behind the stacks of patient charts—go anywhere that took me away from the melee and the responsibility of being a *Doctor*.

That morning wasn't the first time that I had written an order in a patient's chart, but it was the first time that it would not be cosigned by another real, full-fledged doctor. I had written plenty an order as a third-year medical student and then again as a fourth-year. Back then, however, I had flagged the chart because those orders needed to be cosigned. Somebody would have my back. I would be protected. No more.

Now it was all me, mine for the taking. Mine to do correctly—or not. The stakes were high. That sunlight suddenly felt really warm, my white coat heavy, the stethoscope tight around my neck. I had a fleeting thought of a noose. What if I wrote the wrong order? What if someone followed that wrong order? It wasn't like I was ordering a cup of coffee in the cafeteria. No, this was someone's life. I needed to be present. I needed to be *here*.

I wrote the order. *D/c heparin.* Discontinue heparin. I signed my name. And I was no longer what I had been before.

I can count on one hand the knock-the-breath-out-of-me kind of transformations I have undergone. Writing that first order as a doctor was one such moment. Delivering my children was another. Standing at my father's grave, listening to the rabbi chant the memorial prayers, was another such moment. And making challah has become one of those moments. They all transformed me in their own unique ways, but somewhere along the way, between my patients and the carpools and making dinner night after night and cleaning dirty faces and dirty dishes and just plain being everywhere but *here*, I forgot that I needed to be *here*. Up to my elbows in dough each Friday morning, I began to learn how to be *here* again.

Since I don't use five pounds of flour, my dough doesn't always technically merit me saying the prayer, but I say it anyway. Saying the prayer anchors me, and I insist that the bread tastes better for it. Perhaps my small amount of flour used counts as part of the collective amount of dough that qualifies under halakhic law. Since most Fridays I can be found with at least one other woman in the kitchen making challah, I am sure that together we use the requisite amount of flour. Sometimes, it just takes a village.

In fact, if I am making more than one batch of challah myself, or if I am making challah with others, I usually collect up all of the pieces of dough together and say one prayer. Then I toss them as one lump of dough—again, about the size of an egg—double-wrapped in plastic wrap, into my trashcan. Two points, swish. Perhaps, one day, I'll try to burn this little piece of dough in the oven separately just like my great grandmother Ida used to do. Truthfully, I'm a little scared to do this, but all the more reason to try, right? What if the dough doesn't actually burn? What if it causes a small oven fire? One day I'll get over my trepidation. One day I'll just do it.

I did not grow up saying prayers—any prayers, anywhere. I attended Hebrew school on Sunday mornings, though it contained minimal religion studies, and I actually preferred going to church with friends whenever the opportunity arose. All that pomp and circumstance, the beautiful voices of the choir comingling with the organ, the smell of the incense, the light filtering through the stained glass windows, casting shadows across the sanctuary. And when I would visit them in Baltimore, I especially liked going to Quaker meeting with my grandparents. They had decided to become Quaker when my mother was already grown and out of the house. Have you ever been to a Quaker meeting? There, you just sit quietly for an hour, only standing up to speak (about anything and every-thing) if moved to do so. Some meetings, nobody said *anything* for the full hour. As a child, I couldn't fathom that. Nobody had *anything* to say? I could daydream for an hour? It was so incredible to just sit there, lost in my thoughts, uninterrupted.

I've come a long way since then. I like prayer, I value prayer, and I think it makes a difference. Early in my medical residency training in New York City, a family member of one of my patients asked me to pray with her. She was Catholic and her husband lay dying. Her devotion to her husband, and to her belief that praying for him would help, moved me. I agreed. There we sat, a young physician and an older woman at her husband's bedside. The room dimly lit, the IV machine beeping a rhythmic backdrop to an otherwise eerie quiet.

I continued that practice anytime a patient or a patient's family asked me to pray with them or for them. I felt better for it. And I hope that they did, too. Sometimes I had absolutely nothing to offer a patient or her family in the way of treatment or prognosis, and yet telling them that they were in my thoughts and prayers brought us both a measure of comfort. When my dad died, I was especially touched by those who told me that I was in their prayers, though I didn't appreciate that until after the fact.

I feel that same sense of comfort each Friday when I recite the prayer of *Hafrish Challah*. I am doing *something*. I am connecting to a larger world. Also, it never fails to amuse me that there is a prayer in my religion for absolutely everything. And I mean everything. A prayer when I see a rainbow. A prayer when I hear a clap of thunder. A prayer when I first wake up in the morning, having made it through another night. For all of these, and so much more, there is a specific prayer. So a prayer for a piece of dough, a piece of dough that I am then going to discard? But of course.

I remember other women when I bless the separated piece of dough. I remember women around the world who are making bread today, just like me, and breaking a piece of dough off and double-wrapping it, just like me, and I remember other women I've been blessed to know who are no longer here with me.

I remember my lovely and elegant patient from early in my medical career in New York City; she was younger than I am today as I type this. She came to see me with a cough, nothing more. I had been taught during my medical training that the three most common causes of cough in an outpatient internal medicine practice are asthma, postnasal drip, and gastroesophageal reflux (heartburn). She didn't have asthma. I treated her for postnasal drip, then for reflux, though she had no history of that, either. Lung cancer would be the death of her. She had never smoked. Not even to try it, she told me. She was so young, so beautiful. I held onto her business card for years, because I couldn't bear to know she wasn't there, in her sleek black leather bomber jacket, at her oh-so-cool job downtown.

Or I remember Shari, a friend with children who are all practically the same ages as mine. We sat in many a sandbox together, our children scampering over our outstretched legs. She, too, is no longer here; she died much too young. She is no longer able to get up in the night if one of her children awakes. To this day, every single time a child wakes me up in middle of the night, when I know that I'll be ruined with fatigue the next day, I think of Shari, who doesn't have this opportunity anymore. And it touches me every single time.

I remember these women, and so many more. And I linger over this blessing. I offer my own thanks. I am here. I am (trying to be) present. Never mind the traffic on the 405 here in Los Angeles today, never mind the dirty laundry piling up, never mind the handfuls of dark chocolate chips that I ate yesterday. Never mind. I *get* to remember. *I am here.*

With these memories in mind, I break off a small piece of dough and double-wrap it in plastic wrap. I hold this warm nugget gingerly in one hand. And I recite the prayer out loud, blessing the bread. And then I throw it away. That's right—I get rid of this piece of bread. Historically, women burned this separated piece right then and there. A woman I met in Israel told me that she collects her broken pieces in the freezer and once a year, at Passover, burns the lot of them. Since the Temple doesn't exist anymore and we can't give this piece to the Kohen, the priest, we must destroy it. Burn it, double wrap it, put it in the freezer—pick your preference and just get rid of it.

When writing about this, I remembered hearing a story as a small child about my great-grandmother burning a small piece of bread every Friday. I had always thought the story pure lore. Now I know better. My great-grandmother Ida, an Orthodox Jewish woman from Russia who came to America and raised nine children, made challah every Friday and put a small piece in the kitchen oven each week to burn separately. I never understood why. Now I do. I think of her sometimes on Fridays, which then reminds me of my adored grandfather, and I am connected all over again.

So now that I know the meaning behind all of this, I always separate the challah, blessing the small piece of dough I've separated. Except when I don't. Occasionally I do forget. If I remember later on that I omitted this crucial step, I swear the bread doesn't taste as good. Something is missing. It makes me sad.

I try not to forget.

BAKING

Step Eight:

Shaping the Dough

Punch out dough one more time. Cut the dough into two balls, one for each challah. Then divide each ball into three equal pieces. Roll out each piece, crimp together at the top and braid into a loaf. Place on a greased cookie sheet. Repeat with second ball of dough. You may let the dough rise again at this step.

I like design, both to look at and to make. Each week, I get to design two three-braided challahs. Just like braiding my daughter's hair. I like to roll out the individual strands—now with just my hands, though I used to use a rolling pin. I copy the women I've watched just roll out the dough between their hands into long snakelike strands. Even my son made challah this way on his first trip to Israel. I tried it, but the strands were too oblong, too floppy for me to work comfortably with. I went back to the rolling pin for a bit, until I could master just rolling out the dough with my bare hands. Once I roll the dough out, I create the strand itself by rolling the dough up, much like rolling up a small carpet, like I did so long ago in Montessori preschool, or much like rolling up a piece of wrapping paper, with which I get much practice at each holiday season. I really love beautiful wrapping paper; when I need a quick pick-me-up, I have been known to walk down to our elegant little paper store nearby and purchase a ridiculously expensive sheet of wrapping paper. My collection sits in a corner of a closet. I can barely part with the loose sheets even though they just gather cobwebs. Somehow, I just like knowing they rest up there, a whisper of beauty should I need the reminder.

To make the two three-braided challahs, I divide the ball of dough in half; each half I further divide into three pieces for a total of six pieces. I leave three to the side, and work with the first three to make the first loaf. Through trial and lots of error, I've learned it's best to keep the canister of flour handy: if the surface isn't appropriately floured, the dough might stick when I braid it and this may cause the strands to tear a bit—and then they're not so pretty when they're finally baked. It's all about how they look, right? (On some level, I actually believe that.) I want them to look beautiful later that evening on the Shabbas table. Extra flour easily takes care of that predicament.

The moment of truth occurs when actually braiding the dough. Fortunately, the three-braided challah came easily to me, as I've braided many a pigtail. A quick primer for the non-pigtail braider: crimp the three strands at the top and then fan them out. Take the right strand near the top and cross it over the middle; now it's the new middle strand. Then take the left strand near the top and cross that one over the middle; now it's the new middle strand. Work your way down the strands until you get to the bottom. Here I usually tuck the remaining tail of the last strand underneath the end of the loaf so it stays put. It looks fabulous. I feel like a professional every time!

It seems that I have long appreciated pretty designs. Sitting at table in a nondescript banquet hall in Israel several summers ago, overlooking the Western Wall, a challah-baking rebbetzin captivated me. She was the maestro of challah making. Displayed in front of her, on several industrial sized baking sheets, rested many challahs. Unlike my simple three-braided challahs, though, these came in a variety of shapes and sizes. Just imagine: round challahs, challahs shaped like a bird, six-braided challahs, challahs shaped into napkin-rings, and challahs as pretty little flowers. Best of all, she offered to teach us how to do the same with the dough in front of us. Like kids in a candy store, at least kids at the Play-Doh station, we happily dove in. Some of us rolled out the dough with rolling pins; some of us just used our hands to make long snakes of dough. And then the fun began.

Up until that morning, I had always made three-braided challah. That's what I knew without thinking about it. Those were the challahs that we picked up when we gathered up our children after nursery school on Fridays; those were the challahs I bought from our local artisanal bakery in Cleveland. Those were the challahs I saw pictured online or in textbooks or wherever I looked for a picture of challah.

I knew that different shapes existed, such as round challah at the New Year and pull-apart challah rolls that my mother-in-law sometimes served. I did not know, though, that the different shapes had different meanings. I didn't know that it actually mattered, sometimes, how the challah is shaped. I've long known that there is a time and place for everything; and the shape of challah personifies this.

There really is a time and place for everything. It's not always about me, about what I want and when I want it. At the New Year (*Rosh Hashanah*) and for the start of each new month (*Rosh Chodesh*), women create round-shaped challah. No debate. Circular shapes signify the cycle of life. No beginning, no end, just straight-up continuity. Not going to mess with that, I finally mastered the round challah this year after a few misguided attempts for the last several Rosh Hashanah holidays.

The first try a few years ago consisted of my rolling the dough out into two long snakes, twisting them into a long coiled rope, and then wrapping that up in a circular shape. It worked. Sort of. I couldn't replicate how lovely a similarly rounded challah looked at my local bakery and the inside did not cook all the way through without making the outside too crispy. I had not yet discovered the role of the thermometer for these thicker-shaped challahs.

This year, I took my responsibility more seriously. I researched it, I practiced, and ultimately, I let go of my original method. Getting serious is complicated business. No more two-snake round challahs for me; I used four pieces of dough per challah now. Once rolled out, I spread out the four coils, two by two. Next, I crisscrossed two coils over and under the other two. Now I had a grid: imagine it—almost like a cross or an X shape with two coils sticking out in all four directions. Got that?

Then the fun began: choosing to go counterclockwise the

first time (though you could choose either direction), I crossed one end over the other end of each pair; then reversed direction and did it all over again. Sounds complicated, and the first time the execution frustrated me. But oh, the results looked divine. Pulling the oven door open ever so slowly, I saw inside a perfectly golden round challah with a crisscross pattern on top. Hooked, I made round challahs that entire week for all of our visiting friends and family. Each time, it worked; each time, I couldn't believe it worked.

Week in and week out, though, I usually stick with the traditional three-braid challah. It's straightforward. I can make it with my eyes closed and by now I can make it without giving it my full attention. This allows me to simultaneously focus on the women with whom I bake challah and to think about the person in whose merit I make this week's challah. The three-braided challah cooks so quickly, without a thermometer and careful monitoring. A win-win in my book. The braids look like two arms entwined, a symbol of love. I like that. It gets right to heart of it, no ambiguity.

The Challenge of Six-Braided Challah

Six-braided challah challenges me. It seduces me with its inherent elegance: a six-braided loaf looks like it belongs in a bakery display case, or perhaps on someone else's beautifully set Shabbas table. I like the number six: there are six days in the week, not counting Shabbas; and if you make two six-braided loaves, that adds up to twelve. There are twelve tribes of Israel. And it gets better: six plus twelve is eighteen, and eighteen is the number that corresponds to the Hebrew word *chai*, in English "life" and therefore, to many Jews, a symbol of good luck. Beauty, tribes, and life, all in a six-braided challah.

It took me three Fridays before I could successfully make a six-braided challah. Making it required me to completely *stop*, to just be still. And I'm not just talking about stopping my feet from moving. I'm talking about trying to stop and focus solely on the task at hand—and not for very long, mind you, just a few minutes. Focusing wholly and completely on just *one* thing at any time requires a level of single-minded concentration that often eludes me. Letting go, really letting go for a moment, was not something I practiced. It's like meditation. It's hard to just *stop* on demand, but when you do, it can be transformative.

So there I was on the third Friday in a row, trying to master the six-braided challah yet again. And I was really frustrated with myself: really, how hard could this be? I had stuck a needle into a man's heart as a medical resident to try and save his life. I had made the crew team my freshman year of college after having the dubious honor of being only one of two young women in my graduating high school class not to have lettered in a sport during *all* four years of high school. As a five-months-pregnant physician, still suffering from debilitating morning sickness, I had taken care of a patient the morning of 9/11 in midtown New York City, a woman who had watched people jump out of the burning World Trade Center towers and was understandably traumatized. I have done a lot of hard things. I have been challenged before. Really, how hard could this six-braid be? Turns out it can be pretty hard.

After pinching all six rolled-out strands of dough to-gether at the top, and spreading them out like a fan, I was ready to try again. Now it was time to march, military style, left-right-left-right, down the length of the braid. I took the outer-left strand and crossed it over two stands, laying it down in the middle. Then I took the second strand from the right and placed it over to far left. Then I repeated this again from the left side. All the way down the length of the strands until I had a beautiful braided loaf.

I lost myself in a trance: left right, left right. Before I re-alized it, I had completed the braid. For just a few moments, I had done the impossible. I had shut out all distractions. I had focused on just the task at hand. Enthralled, I stared; the six-braided challah looked so professional. With much practice, I have gotten better at this. Now, I can do the six-braided chal-lah without too much trepidation. But listen carefully, and you'll still catch me quietly chanting *left right, left right.*

I haven't tried it yet, but next Yom Kippur I might make challah in the shape of a hand. This holiday is our religion's most serious, the day that concludes the ten days of awe. On Rosh Hashanah it is written; on Yom Kippur it is inscribed: what will be for the year. Hand-shaped challah symbolizes that we will be inscribed for a good year. I have faith and I will take any added insurance. Or, perhaps, I'll make a ladder-shaped challah. The ladder symbolizes Moses's ascent on Mt. Sinai, so some make this shape pre-Yom Kippur to represent our collective spiritual ascent at this time.

My favorite shape I learned in Israel from the rebbetzin: the bird-shaped challah roll. It really looks like a bird. Much has been written as to what the bird shape signifies. I just like making them, their intense symbolism an added bonus. One of my favorite Jewish cookbook authors, Joan Nathan, has written that the protective meaning of this shape is derived from Isaiah 31:5: "As birds hovering [over their fledglings], so will the Lord of hosts protect Jerusalem." Another food writer/historian, Gil Marks, has written that they symbolize that "our sins should fly away and . . . our prayers soar to the heavens." That's rather auspicious at the holiday time, don't you think?

A bird is made with just one coil of dough. Take the coil and tie it into a knot. At one end, you can place two raisins, cranberries, or maybe currants for the eyes of the bird. Whatever moves you, whatever you have in your pantry that day. At the other end, take a knife and cut two small slices and fan these out slightly, to make a tail shape. Voila, you have a bird.

Other holidays have their own special affiliated challah shapes: small, triangular-shaped challah for Purim, a Jewish holiday that commemorates the day the Jews narrowly escaped a genocide plotted by the evil Haman. The triangle symbolizes Haman's hat. For Shavuos, the day that the Jews received the Ten Commandments on Mt. Sinai, some bakers create a challah with two long strands that are attached side-by-side, symbolizing the Tablets of Law.

And just for the beauty of it, I like to make little flower rolls. Roll out one strand of dough, and then tie it up like a mini-pretzel. It's sweet and lovely to look at when it's baked. I sometimes make these when I have rolled out uneven strands of dough. They also make an entertaining and unexpected little gift for someone.

BAKING

Step Nine:

Painting the Dough

Paint each challah with a mixture of egg yolk plus a little water.

After shaping the dough the way that I want to for that particular Friday, I place it on an oiled baking sheet. Now, time to paint, as my daughter affectionately calls it. No smock required. An egg yolk mixed with a bit of water makes for a great glaze. The glaze *finishes* the dough for me, much like setting a visually appealing table for Shabbas dinner, or adding a piece of jewelry to an outfit. Much like remembering to put on lipstick when I was a younger physician. Patients, and sometimes their family members, constantly said that I couldn't possibly be old enough to be a doctor and I believed that if I put on lipstick, I would somehow suddenly morph into an older-appearing doctor, a wiser doctor; and interestingly enough, when I did remember to put on lipstick (MAC lip care, Satin Lipstick, Color Twig), fewer people questioned my age, my ability, my right to be a physician.

I use just one egg yolk per batch. I used to mindlessly toss the unused egg white down the garbage disposal. For years, I never thought to save that lone egg white. Week in and week out, I tossed it out. How many egg whites did I waste? Making challah is a process, and as such, I am constantly editing the process. Making several batches of challah at once a few years ago, I realized that I was about to dispose of several perfectly good handpicked farmers' market egg whites. My hand poised high above the disposal, I froze midair, and then reversed course. Every week now I save them. One egg or two, or however many I use that week. Now, on Saturday mornings, my husband or one of our kids makes leftover challah French toast for the kids, and my husband uses the leftover egg white to make a great omelet.

Happiness

Some people are just born happy, or perhaps they just choose to be happy. And some are not born happy, and don't necessarily choose to be so. Some patients always smiled when I walked into their examination room. Maybe they had easily found a parking spot. Maybe their blood pressure wasn't too high when it was checked moments before I walked in. Maybe they knew that they weren't going to get any shots that day. Maybe they were just happy to see me. Maybe they got to do something that day that brought them happiness. Or maybe they were faking it. A rabbi we once studied with said, "Fake it till you make it. After all, actions speak louder than words." Just act happy even if you're not, and after a while, you'll probably feel better. He wasn't talking about happiness, per se, but I've taken the liberty of generalizing some of his teachings and in the process, have found myself in a much better place.

We can't always be happy. Sometimes happiness is taken from us. Sometimes terrible things really do go bump in the night. While painting challah with a red-tipped brush may seem childish, may seem frivolous, I look forward to this with almost too much glee. In fact, whenever possible, I insist on doing this step myself, instead of handing it over to a child or a friend or anyone else. I want the reminder. I want the physical reminder that when we have the choice to be happy, we have to grab it. We have to take it and own and cherish it. It is not always ours to choose.

I choose to paint with abandon. I choose to splatter the egg yolk wash every which way, covering not only the challah dough but also some of the baking sheet itself and even managing to get the countertop with a few droplets. I choose happiness when I can; I've seen just how ephemeral it can be.

SIDEBAR: The Pastry Brush

The Pastry Brush. My first pastry brush was a traditional one. I bought it at our local grocery store because the price was right and I was in a hurry. Not a very wise move.

That first brush had a thick wooden handle, and was loaded with sharp bristles. Actual bristles: I assume they were acrylic, or some such synthetic material, though I don't really know.

It reminded me of an old paintbrush sitting in our laundry room, all wooden handle and thick bristles. I do know, though, that this brush was not very effective: occasionally, I found bristles on the dough as I glazed it. Perhaps as a result of studying salmonella in medical school, or perhaps as a result of treating someone with a salmonella infection as a resident, but I have a lingering fear of raw eggs. Thus, having to pick out bristles from the glaze on top of the dough was not only a sticky endeavor, but also a stressful one.

Fortunately, I shortly thereafter discovered the brush that I still use today. The one that I made sure made the move across the country with us, marked by the movers so that I could find it that first Friday in our new home. It's a small, bright red silicone pastry brush: so cute, it makes me smile. Comfortable to hold, this brush is easy to manipulate across the dough, as though we have been longtime friends. I love how the bristles swish back and forth, and how they stay attached to the brush, exactly where they belong. Yes, it's just a little red pastry brush, but actually so much more.

Step Ten:

Baking the Challah

Place on a greased baking sheet and bake approximately 23-30 minutes, or until bread has risen and is golden brown. Remove, let cool.

The original recipe said to bake the challah for approximately forty-five minutes or until golden brown. After approximately twenty-five minutes, I peeked. I couldn't resist the aroma wafting through my kitchen. I had no patience. Two golden loaves stared back at me. I stared right back, so stunned—they looked just like the pictures I had ogled; they looked better than what I had seen displayed in the grocery store. I carefully removed them and turned off the oven. Since that day, I have never baked three-braided challah for more then 25-30 minutes.

I just bake the bread until it's done. "Done" is difficult to explain; it is perhaps the hardest step in the recipe to articulate. Twenty-five minutes in my oven won't necessarily be twenty-five minutes in your oven. "Done" reflects so many factors, some tangible and some not. Perhaps it's the quality of the ingredients I've used that day, perhaps it's the weather or what's in the air that day. You don't need complicated tools to quantify the degree of doneness. No thermometers, no tapping the bottom, listening and feeling for the telltale signs—just trust, pure and simple. Trust that when it looks golden brown and smells wonderful, it's done.

One day around the Jewish New Year (I remember the time of year because the challah I had made that night had a round shape), I made my coils, made my round challahs, painted and baked as usual, and pulled out this rounded challah suffused with a heavenly aroma, as usual. I received appreciative glances from our guests, as usual. Our company that evening included an older woman close to my mother's age. She was an elegant and intelligent woman, a woman I wanted to impress. Alas, the center of the challah was not fully baked. It was soft, yeasty dough and almost raw. She was gracious, but I was mortified.

I went back to the books. I read about baking bread, about using thermometers in this regard. Touch, smell, feel: time to use my senses. Time to be sensible. The bread may not need forty-five minutes to bake thoroughly through, but I had been cavalier. Different shapes required different baking times. Perhaps even different temperatures.

I tried a slightly lower temperature and a longer baking time for the six-braided challah. It was so much larger than a mere three-braid, so much denser. I actually broke out the old cooking thermometer buried in the back of the utensil drawer in the kitchen—the thermometer I had never used, but had carried with me through multiple moves, multiple cities. Had it known that decades later I would need it? The round challah or a six-braided challah needs to reach over 190° before I remove it from the oven. Now I know better. Now I have greater patience.

If I had only listened when I was younger, if only I had tried to learn more patience, I might have made better challah sooner. I might have done many things sooner. I might have had more patience for my patients sometimes. Sometimes when I was overwhelmed and frustrated, I thought, "Why can't they just hurry up and get better, faster?"

The osteoporotic that wouldn't do any weight-bearing exercise. The overweight diabetic I often saw in the hospital cafeteria, refilling a large soda cup. The one with a sexually transmitted disease who refused to use condoms. All of them who didn't complete their antibiotic regimens, yet always seemed to call in for them after hours, setting my beeper to vibrate at strange times during the night.

Sometimes I am noncompliant, too. Sometimes I don't follow my doctor's advice. Sometimes I eat too much or not enough. Sometimes I forego sleep. Or don't take medicine for a headache soon enough. Sometimes I just want everyone else to do as I say, not as I do. It is ironic, the doctor who doesn't want to be a patient, or even just be patient.

But then the bread doesn't bake properly. All that effort, for naught.

I want the bread to come out perfectly. Therefore, sometimes I have to call in reinforcements. I know now approximately how long to bake the bread to get the end result that I desire. I know now what I want. I just don't always know how to get there. At those times, I call in Carmen.

Carmen helps our family on Fridays. I didn't appreciate

the significance of the day of the week that she helps us until she began to take the challah out of the oven for me. I could tell her approximately what time it should be done, but she could always tell exactly when. *How*, I wondered. How did she get it right every time?

"The smell," she told me. One moment, it is just bread baking in the oven. And the next moment, as though a switch has been flipped, it metamorphoses into *challah*. The whole house becomes infused with the aroma. Wherever Carmen is in our home, she knows when the bread has finished baking. And she's right every time.

SIDEBAR: The Pastry Cutter

The Pastry Cutter. I don't pull this handy little tool out until I've finished braiding the dough, until my work on the kitchen counter is complete. This instrument makes me feel like a legitimate baker, but I don't use it in the preparation of my bread. I use it to clean up. I use it to scrape the excess dough off the counter while the challah bakes. It's clean, efficient. And much better than my first pastry cutter, an inexpensive plastic one, that succumbed to too many cycles in the dishwasher. My current pastry cutter has a thick white handle and metal blade. It cuts sharply across the countertop. Now you see the mess, now you don't. The flour and the bits of dough rapidly disappear.

BAKING

Step Eleven:

Rituals Around Eating Challah

Place challah on platter, cover, and wait for Shabbas dinner. Eat and enjoy!

My friend Hillary relies on the concept of *Hiddur Mitzvah*; I don't know whether she does so consciously or not. Perhaps I should ask her. Regardless, *Hiddur Mitzvah* describes beautifying a mitzvah by appealing to our senses, of going above and beyond the formal demands of the mitzvah. She has not only made fabulous-tasting challah for us, but she also made it look like a work of art. Arriving at our home for Shabbas, she carried challah beautifully wrapped, like the gift it is meant to be. This package reminded me, again, that I could do good—do a good deed—just by making something more beautiful, that this was not a trivial action.

Before we eat the challah later that evening, I try my own hand now at *Hiddur Mitzvah*: one of us covers the two challahs that we place on the dinner table with a rich tapestry of a challah cover, purchased in Israel for just this purpose. I purchased this ornate, richly patterned challah cover because of the importance of covering challah. Not just because it looks beautiful (it does). Not just because it lends a festive, celebratory air to the dinner table (it does). Rather, this cover is a stand-in, a reminder to us that when the Israelites wandered in the desert for forty years, subsisting on manna, they found this manna covered in a protective dew so that it didn't dry out. My challah cover substitutes for the dew. Protected, guarded, safe for the Shabbas meal later that evening.

No one touches any of the finished, warm challah until Shabbas dinner. No sneaking a taste, a crumb. We might look at the loaves just sitting there, waiting to be tasted; we might ogle them while they cool, before covering them. One of us may want a taste. But we wait. When I buy a baguette, it doesn't usually make it into our house before one of us has eaten the tip, the Pope's nose. And I think nothing of taking a piece of sourdough bread out of the grocery bag on the way home from the farmer's market, unceremoniously, and having a nibble. But my relationship with challah is different. I wait (im)patiently to try it.

When dinnertime arrives, and everyone gathers around the table, we say three prayers. I usually say the first, lighting the candles, sometimes with any other women present who also wish to participate. The time has been predetermined according to the time of sunset. It should be before sunset, no later than eighteen minutes after the pre-determined candle-lighting time, technically. Lighting candles blesses our home, bringing peace to all of us. Selfishly, I think it brings peace more to me: as I finish the prayer, and bring my hands together in front of my heart, I always pause, inhale deeply, look around at my children, and utter, "Good Shabbas."

Sometimes they laugh in recognition, "Mom, you *always* say that. You always turn and look at us just like [with dramatic pause] *that*." They're right. Yet somehow, as I say those two words, I *am* always overcome with a sense of peace, of rightness, of this-is-where-I-belong. It's a lovely feeling.

(Candles)
Transliteration: Barukh atah Adonai Eloheinu melekh ha'olam asher kid'shanu b'mitzvotav v'tzivanu l'hadlik ner shel shabbat.

Translation: Blessed are You, Lord our God, Ruler of the Universe, who has sanctified us with commandments, and commanded us to light Shabbat candles.

The candles will burn throughout dinner and beyond. They will burn until they burn themselves out. We don't blow them out. Everything is fabulous in the right light.

We bless the wine next. Some of our friends have beautiful, decorative wine fountains: a larger kiddush cup sits on top of a contraption with eight to twelve mini-cups in a circle beneath it. It looks like a layered, tiered cake. When wine is poured into the larger kiddush cup, it overflows and fills the smaller cups. It's a real crowd-pleaser.

(Wine)
Transliteration: Barukh ata Adonai Eloheinu melekh ha'olam borei p'ri hagafen.

Translation: Blessed are You, Lord our God, Ruler of
the universe, who creates the fruit of the vine.

And then the moment that we've all anticipated: the time
to say the blessing before eating the challah. Another friend
of ours used to stand up at the head of his Shabbas table, pick
up the two loaves and resoundingly clap them together. If we
remember, we copy him. This is a fabulous way to begin the
blessing: it's so dramatic, so fun. Then we say the prayer—actually, we usually ask one of the kids (ours or someone else's,
doesn't matter) present to start us off.

(Challah)
Transliteration: Barukh ata Adonai Eloheinu melekh
ha'olam hamotzi lehem min ha'aretz.

Translation: Blessed are You, Lord our God, Ruler of
the universe, who brings forth bread from the earth.

Our true colors emerge, then: I like to pull the challah
apart to serve it. Really rip it. My husband likes to slice the
challah. Most of our friends are the slicing type, too. Wonder
what that says about me. Anyway, usually we end up slicing it
for everyone at the table. And when we're really on our
game, we have a little bit of salt handy. The Shabbas table is a
substitute for the altar at the Temple; salt was always offered
with sacrifices there, so it's appropriate that we use it now.
And I just think it's ridiculously cool, a few dramatic dips of
challah into a small bowl of salt. It looks special, so it is special. I am still looking for just the right saltcellar. For a long

time, I thought of obtaining an elaborate, silver saltcellar—reminiscent of something baroque, ancient, European; something decadent. Recently, I have been eyeing a sleek, modern little light wooden saltcellar, Scandinavian. Perhaps I'll purchase it. Perhaps not. Sometimes it's just a relief to have something frivolous to think about.

At Rosh Hashanah, the Jewish New Year, we also get out our honey pot. (As an aside, no salt dipping at Rosh Hashanah, just honey dipping.) As challah dipped in honey remains truly one of life's divine experiences, we often put out this little pot of honey for several weeks in a row at this time, so seduced are we by the sweetness of the honey comingled with the challah. Our little pot is a silver-plated, apple-shaped vessel, as in the apples and honey that we always serve at Rosh Hashanah for a sweet new year. I couldn't resist purchasing it from the Skirball Museum just after we moved to Los Angeles. Although I never buy anything at museum gift shops as a rule, I felt moved that day to make a purchase. I thought that I should add to our paltry Judaica collection. And this pot just looks so beautiful; I was captivated.

Thank goodness for that impulse purchase: challah dipped in honey is one of earth's finest pleasures—I wish that I remembered to put this honey pot out more often.

But back to the bread.

Pieces of challah are distributed around the table.

And then *nothing*. Just the quiet sounds of everyone eating challah.

The serving platter empties, one loaf gone in a flash. I escape to the kitchen to bring in the rest of the meal. Sometime later, the second loaf will likely be eaten, too, between the laughter and the chatter, the multiple conversations, the adults and the children and everyone in between. Another week lived.

CONCLUSION

I became a doctor, a clinician trained in internal medicine, with a practice in women's health and wellness. Now I practice a different medicine. Before, I felt marionette-like, a puppet on a larger stage. Before, I practiced a medicine others wanted me to practice. Now, I practice a different kind of medicine, more authentic for me, one of my choosing. After much reflection, after trying on a few different white coats to see what fit, I stopped relying on just pharmacology to treat my patients and instead began to also rely on food (*farm*-acy, not so much *pharm*-acy). And simultaneously, for my patients and for myself, it became more than just eating the right foods, although that helps—a lot. It also became about taking a moment to slow down, to be aware, to be here.

Now I prescribe making challah, not just cholesterol-lowering pills. Now I prescribe breathing, not just beta-blockers. And I believe it works as well—in fact, I believe sometimes it works even better. Especially when the challah is warm to the touch (and taste!), just out of the oven, steam curling up from its inside. Of course, it's not pills or no pills, challah or not. It's appreciating the balance, that there can be more than *one* way.

I found in making challah that the magic for me is in the *process* of making challah. No ends-justify-the-means here. What happened as I went through the eleven steps each Friday in this challah recipe is where I really learned to be present. To slow down for a moment each week. To appreciate the here and now. To reconnect with other women. I found through these eleven steps that challah is the ultimate *soul* food for me.

It was here all the time, I just didn't see it. I was so concerned with doing the right thing all the time, being the right person at the right time, that I had unknowingly lost the enjoyment, the fabulousness of the here and now.

And it was there all the time, I just didn't recognize it: the need to help others from an early age. I learned Braille at age eight and then wrote a cookbook for the blind; I took a cooking class in Paris one day when I was fourteen, alone and an ocean away from my family, obsessed even then with food. It was always all there: the knowledge that *food is medicine*. The best kind of medicine. Whether writing a pamphlet about eating disorders in my late teens for our local children's hospital, or working as medical director for a program to treat chronic disease through lifestyle modification, it was always there in my life.

I didn't realize that, really, it's okay to stop, to get messy in a bowl of dough. In fact, it's better than okay. It's just what the doctor ordered. Want to feel better? Want your blood pressure to go down, want your moods to stabilize, want your risk of cancer to lessen? Just *stop*. Hit the pause button. For me, it's making challah on Fridays, preferably with other women. But no matter. Maybe your thing is to read a book. Or maybe it's to volunteer or to go for a hike or to snap a photo. At the core of what I've learned these past ten years and over one thousand challahs and over one thousand patients later is this fundamental truism: it's within all of us to make a choice to *be present*.

It doesn't matter how we express that choice. Just acknowledge the choice. We get one life, and one life only. While writing the last chapters of this book, a childhood friend of my brother's dropped dead of a massive heart attack. He left behind two children the approximate ages of two of my children. And a wife. And so much more. I made challah in his merit that week. I remembered when he had come over to our house to play when we were kids. I hugged my children extra tight that night.

Everything that we do is a choice. Even when we do nothing, that is a choice. I didn't always realize this simple fact. Now I do. It is so obvious in hindsight. Running through hospital corridors, writing out yet another prescription for a patient's chronic disease, or pushing a swing back and forth for the millionth time at the playground, I didn't realize in the midst of that maelstrom that I had a choice. That I had made a choice—and I could make another, different choice.

So I made a choice to make challah.

Whether you choose the life you have now, or want something different, it's yours to choose. You can reclaim your *self*, perhaps one lopsided braid of dough at a time.

Sometimes it's still difficult to change behavior—to slow down and be *here*—though less so the longer I am at this. I know that I am not alone. Behavioral change is hard work. But behavior *can* be changed. I have seen it done firsthand. For example, I have spent a lot of time with my patients encouraging them to exercise each day—to just move their bodies each and every day—and that advice often fell on deaf ears. They gave too many excuses to count, but sometimes I got through.

There was one woman I remember in particular who did

try to exercise each day, a little bit here, a little bit there. It really doesn't matter; it doesn't have to be thirty minutes all at once. Ten minutes here and ten minutes there add up quite quickly. And the most amazing thing happened: this patient kept doing it. It's been said that if you do something for twenty-eight days, chances are you'll do it on the twenty-ninth. If you can walk, for example, every day for a month, research shows that your odds of continuing to walk after that dramatically improve. My patient did it. If you only walk for fifteen days and stop, then you might not start up again. My patient kept walking long past twenty-eight days. She kept walking until she had walked her diabetes right into the ground. She went off insulin. She no longer had to stick her finger multiple times a day to check her sugar levels. The constant and unrelenting presence of her feet pounding on the pavement was the end to that dreaded diagnosis. A behavior changed.

I started making challah every Friday. And kept making it, for twenty-eight Fridays and beyond. Now I have changed my behavior. Now I try to make challah no matter what. It's an ingrained behavior; I just figure out how to get it done each Friday. It used to be a real struggle, but not so much anymore. It's become a habit—which, after all, is just a fancy word for a behavior changed. It's become living proof that I can adapt, I can slow down, I can be present, every Friday. Well . . . almost every Friday.

Everything comes full circle. In medical school, a favorite expression that our teachers often intoned: *See one, do one, teach one.* And some days, that's exactly what happened. When I was an intern, I watched my resident perform a paracentesis (removal of fluid from the abdominal cavity) from a patient with cirrhosis (a chronic disease of the liver that often results from hepatitis or alcoholism). Several days later, when the patient needed the procedure again, it was my turn to do the honors. Remarkably, my hand was steady as I inserted the needle in his abdomen. Remarkably, he let me. And sure enough, several days later, it was my turn to teach our third-year medical student while my resident stood close by, supervising us. Everything comes full circle. Here I can be found every Friday, spoon in hand, making challah, usually teaching a friend or two or more.

Running late today, out of flour, I fumbled in the checkout line at the local grocery store when my phone rang. Rachel was making challah herself, at home, using the recipe we had used in my kitchen several weeks ago. She had made the yeast mixture, and had a question about adding the remaining ingredients in the first mix. The phone call made me so happy; I danced in the confines of the small checkout line, fist-bumping the gangly, acne-faced young checkout man who probably thought I was just some crazy middle-aged lady. *See one, do one, teach one.* I bet Rachel will soon be teaching someone how to make her own challah, just as soon as she espies that gorgeous challah currently baking in her own oven.

Dana is another such friend. I dropped off a small container of yeast along with the recipe at her front door, and now she makes challah more frequently, especially to have enough for Saturday morning French toast, a big hit in her family. Recently, Dana made challah for a group Shabbas dinner and now all those women want her to teach them how to make challah. She will come back over to my kitchen to learn a few more braiding techniques and then she will teach them—and now the circle is complete. She came, she saw, she conquered. All from a container of yeast.

And as for that second loaf of challah I sometimes make? What is better than the smell of challah French toast emanating from the kitchen the next morning, your child's pajamas splattered with ingredients, the kitchen counter much too messy for an ordinary breakfast, and there, standing in front of the stove, your child with an apron askew, trying valiantly to make breakfast?

Leftover Challah French Toast—
Made by children or others not interested in exact measurements

Sliced challah
2 eggs, for approx. half a loaf of challah
Generous splash of milk
Dollop of vanilla
Squirt of honey
Few shakes of cinnamon

1. Mix all ingredients except challah slices in large baking dish.

2. Coat both sides of challah slices in egg mixture.

3. Melt butter in frying pan on stove, heated to medium.

4. Place soaked challah slices in frying pan; brown both sides—leave in for desired crispness.

5. Serve immediately; maple syrup, powdered sugar or sliced bananas are nice additions on top.

The act of making the bread—mixing and kneading, watching and waiting—can heal your heartache and your emptiness, your sense of being overwhelmed; it did for me. You could bake bread once a week, every week. I did. You can make it alone or with other women, like Rachel and Dana have done. The smell of fresh baking bread turned our house into a home. So go ahead, get down those ingredients, grab a bowl, and call me in the morning. I'd love to hear how you're doing.

ACKNOWLEDGMENTS

If the countless patients I encountered in medical school, residency, and in my practice hadn't been so generous and courageous and inspiring, there wouldn't be a book.

If Wesley Hogan hadn't encouraged me for years to write down these medical stories that kept burbling up inside of me, there wouldn't be a book.

If Abby Rothschild hadn't called me just before the holidays so long ago and encouraged me to try and make a challah, there wouldn't be a book.

If I hadn't been able to make challah almost every Friday since then, often with a rotating cast of women (some are mentioned in the book, some are not, though all hold a sacred spot in my heart), there wouldn't be a book.

If Maria Chavez hadn't been there to take the challah out of the oven sometimes so I could pick up the children from school, there wouldn't be a book.

If Chana Heller and Lana Rizika and Talia Resin hadn't encouraged me to go on a Jewish Women's Renaissance Program Trip to Israel, there wouldn't be a book.

If Emily Greenspan hadn't introduced me to Sam Polk, who suggested that I be in touch with Jennie Nash, who became my trusted book coach, there wouldn't be a book—or even the idea of a book.

If Sharon Shenker, who first taught me so much about the history of challah, and Tracey Alexander hadn't both been early instrumental readers, there wouldn't be a book.

If it weren't for my publishing team at She Writes Press, including Brooke Warner and Lauren Wise, and for my publicity and marketing team at SparkPoint Studio, including Crystal Patriarche and Tabitha Bailey, there wouldn't have been a book.

If it weren't for my family, my parents, and siblings, who have always encouraged me, supported me, and eaten my challah with joy, there wouldn't be a book.

And, most importantly, if it weren't for the unending deep and abiding love and support of my husband and children, there never would have been a second challah made—and there definitely wouldn't be a book.

For all of you, I am most grateful.

About the Author

photo credit: Gary Marschka

BETH RICANATI, MD has built her career around bringing wellness into women's everyday lives, especially busy moms juggling life and children. She received her medical training at Case Western Reserve University and New York-Presbyterian/ Columbia University Medical Center. She was a practicing physician for over ten years at both the New York-Presbyterian/Columbia University Medical Center's Women Health Center in New York City, the Cleveland Clinic's Center for Women's Health, and the Cleveland Clinic's Wellness Institute. She now lives in the Los Angeles area with her family and challah-loving dog.

Follow her on:
Website: www.housecallsforwellness.com
Instagram: www.instagram.com/housecallsforwellness
Facebook: www.facebook.com/BethRicanatiAuthor

SELECTED TITLES FROM SHE WRITES PRESS

She Writes Press is an independent publishing company
founded to serve women writers everywhere.
Visit us at www.shewritespress.com.

Raw by Bella Mahaya Carter. $16.95, 978-1-63152-345-8. In an
effort to holistically cure her chronic stomach problems, Bella Mahaya
Carter adopted a 100 percent raw, vegan diet—a first step on a
quest that ultimately dragged her, kicking and screaming, into
spiritual adulthood.

Learning to Eat Along the Way by Margaret Bendet. $16.95, 978-1-
63152-997-9. After interviewing an Indian holy man, newspaper
reporter Margaret Bendet follows him in pursuit of enlightenment
and ends up facing demons that were inside her all along.

Painting Life: My Creative Journey Through Trauma by Carol K.
Walsh. $16.95, 978-1-63152-099-0. Carol Walsh was a psycho-
therapist working with traumatized clients when she encountered
her own traumatic experience; this is the story of how she used
creativity and artistic expression to heal, recreate her life, and ultimately thrive.

Renewable: One Woman's Search for Simplicity, Faithfulness, and Hope
by Eileen Flanagan. $16.95, 978-1-63152-968-9. At age forty-nine,
Eileen Flanagan had an aching feeling that she wasn't living up to
her youthful ideals or potential, so she started trying to change the
world—and in doing so, she found the courage to change her life.

Rethinking Possible: A Memoir of Resilience by Rebecca Faye Smith
Galli. $16.95, 978-1-63152-220-8. After her brother's devastatingly
young death tears her world apart, Becky Galli embarks upon a quest
to recreate the sense of family she's lost—and learns about healing
and the transformational power of love over loss along the way.

*The Art of Play: Igniting Your Imagination to Unlock Insight, Healing,
and Joy* by Joan Stanford. $19.95, 978-1-63152-030-3. Lifelong
"non-artist" Joan Stanford shares the creative process that led her to
insight and healing, and shares ways for others to do the same.